The Foundations of Tibetan Buddhism

His Eminence Kalu Rinpoche wearing the ceremonial Gampopa Hat
Photograph taken at Kagyu Ling Retreat Center, Plaige France

THE FOUNDATIONS OF TIBETAN BUDDHISM

The Gem Ornament of Manifold Oral Instructions
Which Benefits Each and Everyone Accordingly

H. E. KALU RINPOCHE

Snow Lion Publications
Ithaca, NY USA

Snow Lion Publications
P.O. Box 6483
Ithaca, New York 14851 USA
tel. 607-273-8519

Printed in Canada on acid-free, recycled paper.

ISBN   1-55939-117-0

Library of Congress Cataloging-in-Publication Data

Karma-raṅ-byuṅ-kuṅ-khyab-'phrin-las, Khenpo Kalu.
The foundations of tibetan buddhism.

1. Spiritual life (Buddhism) 2. Buddhism–China–Tibet–Doctrines.
3. Kar-ma-pa (Sect)–Doctrines.

I. Title.
BQ7775.K37   1987   294.3'444   87-20650
ISBN   1-55939-117-0

CONTENTS

Editor's Preface   7
Acknowledgments   9
Foreword   11

1. The Three Yanas   13
2. Ordinary Preliminary Practices   31
3. Ngöndro: Refuge and Prostrations   47
4. Ngöndro: Dorje Sempa Meditation   57
5. Ngöndro: Mandala Practice   63
6. Ngöndro: Guru Yoga Practice and
   Guru-Disciple Relationship   73
7. Lay Vows   89
8. The Bodhisattva Vow   103
9. Vajrayana Commitment and
   the Fourteen Root Downfalls   113
10. Shamatha Practice: Object Meditation   127
11. Shamatha Practice: Objectless Meditation   143
12. Four Causes Leading to Rebirth in Dewachen   157
13. Mahamudra   163
14. Concluding Remarks   173

Glossary   189
Bibliography   195
Dedication   197

The Gem Ornament of Manifold Oral Instructions Which Benefits Each and Everyone Appropriately

I go for refuge to the divine assemblies of the Three Jewels
  and Three Roots. Please grant us your blessings.
All sentient beings of the six kinds who have been our parents,
Who are bound in the state of cyclic existence due to self-clinging,
Who, by their not having comprehended taking rebirth endlessly,
Are distracted by concerns of this life only,
I pity the distress of their pain and separation at the time of death.
From virtuous and nonvirtuous actions, one experiences the results
  as bliss and suffering.
By this nectar of oral instructions which point out this situation
To all sentient beings who are confused as in a dream,
Having sown in their mind streams the seed of liberation,
And having in the end freed them from samsaric suffering,
I have written this for the purpose of attaining the state of
  Buddhahood,
Permanent Bliss.

EDITOR'S PREFACE

A book of this nature challenges the boundaries of the mind. As editors, we read a text many times over, and what has struck us forcefully is the perfected clarity of Rinpoche's presentation. He makes the idea of transforming our limiting mental constructs seem quite logical and attainable.

There are so few Tibetan Buddhist texts available in Western languages that we must rely on the visits and oral teachings of each lineage holder to bring us the living Dharma. The cycle of teachings in this book was delivered by His Eminence Kalu Rinpoche at a meditation retreat in Marcola, Oregon, USA, in 1982.

We were fortunate to hear those teachings, so it is a special privilege to see them into print. In a small way, this translation from oral to written carries on the tradition of transmitting the Dharma from one culture to another.

We are grateful to Lama Lodö for his knowledge and patience as our advisor on this project; he has unstintingly given his time and expertise. Lama Lodö's devotion to his teacher, Kalu Rinpoche, has also been a powerful example to us.

It is His Eminence Kalu Rinpoche's compassion that has brought Lama Lodö and his brother lamas to the West. We are indebted to his generosity and their guidance.

May this book benefit all beings.

Caroline M. Parke (Karma Yeshe Chödrön)
Nancy J. Clark (Karma Pema Zangmo)
Eugene, Oregon

In Appreciation

We wish to express our appreciation to Lama Chökyi Nyima for his wonderful translation of His Eminence Kalu Rinpoche's teachings. He originally met with the Dharma in Vancouver, B.C., where he took refuge with Lama Tsewang Jurme. Through the help of various lamas and scholars, he thoroughly learned the Tibetan language. In time, he participated in one of the three-year retreats in France and then was the personal translator for His Eminence Kalu Rinpoche for a time. His personal experience in practice and his very clear understanding of the Tibetan language have made this book possible. Our heartfelt thanks go out to him.

KDK Publications
July 1986

ACKNOWLEDGMENTS

This book is the result of many people's efforts. The transcribers of the taped lectures upon which this book is based were Susan Millemann (Karma Trinley Zangmo), Catherine Travis (Karma Dawa Lhamo), Ruthanne Harris (Karma Tabka Pema), Allen Carosio (Karma Chöying Gyatso), Karen Nelson (Karma Chökyi Dronma), Douglas Margell (Karma Dawa Zangpo), and Emmy Fox (Karma Sönam Lhatso).

The manuscript was typed and copyedited by Dr. Corina Meyer (Karma Pema Khandro) on a word processor whose use was donated by Joe West (Karma Kungha Namgyal). Early manuscript review was done by Bil Voigt (Karma Jinpa Tarchin) and Bill Velton (Karma Tashi Nyima). Proofreading was done by Alexis Kostich. The glossary was compiled by Michael Conklin (Karma Sönam Rinchen). The editors were Caroline Parke (Karma Yeshe Chodron) and Nancy Clark (Karma Pema Zangmo).Kira Henriksen (Karma Sönam Chötso) was the liaison between KDK and the editors.

The Vajrayogini line drawing was done by Cynthia Moku (Karma Lodö Zangmo); and the Mandala drawing by Elizabeth Johnson (Karma Sönam Chötso).

A generous donation by John P. Staubo of Karma Tashi Ling in Oso, Norway, made the first edition of this book possible.

I wish to thank each of these individuals for their dedicated work and Snow Lion Publications for bringing out this latest edition.

Lama Lodö
San Francisco

Venerable Lama Lodö, His Eminence Kalu Rinpoche, and Very Venerable Bokar
Rinpoche at the River Ganges at Benares, India
© *Küntzang Trinley*

FOREWORD

I bow down in heartfelt devotion to His Eminence Vajradhara Kalu Rinpoche, who is the embodiment of countless Buddhas and Bodhisattvas.

This book contains fourteen chapters dealing with aspects of the path to enlightenment as explained by His Eminence Kalu Rinpoche. The perspective is Buddhist in general, with teachings from the scriptures of the Theravadin, Mahayana, and Vajrayana traditions. H.E. Kalu Rinpoche is recognized by the lineage holders of the four major schools in Tibet as a meditation master equal in stature to the great Yogi Milarepa. Since his approach is nonsectarian, the teachings can be of benefit to anyone from any tradition. He has also been recognized by His Holiness Gyalwa Karmapa and the Great Khyentse Rinpoche (Chökyi Lodö) as the activity emanation of Jamgon Kongtrul the Great, who was also a nonsectarian teacher.

Long ago, an Indian sage said that while Tibetans spent their lives practicing hundreds of traditions and accomplishing none of them, Indian people spent their lives practicing only one but accomplishing them all. The Tibetans learned from this criticism, and H.E. Kalu Rinpoche, like Jamgon Kongtrul the Great, His Holiness Karmapa, and other great masters, attained enlightenment through devoting all his energies to the practice of the teachings of one lineage—not through diluting his efforts by practicing a little here and a little there. These teachers were like the mountain climber who sees many paths to the top of the mountain, but gets to the top by one path. From the top, and while standing in one place, they see the validity of all the other paths ascending the mountain.

It is important for the reader to understand what is meant when I say that these great teachers were nonsectarian. It does not mean that the teachings of the various lineages and schools were mixed together, taught, and practiced with disregard for their separate integrity. Rather, it means that each tradition is regarded as a correct, valid, and important path in its own right, and that no preference or favoritism was shown for one over the other. It is similar to driving a car to a distant place. As a "nonsectarian" driver you understand that any car can and will get you to the destination—you don't even have a preference. This does not mean that you will stupidly attempt to drive more than one car at a time, which would surely result in your not attaining the goal.

Since 1974, H.E. Kalu Rinpoche has established hundreds of centers all over the world. These centers are not in existence by name alone, but are actual sources of the tradition, usually by virtue of a resident lama placed there by Rinpoche. Many of the centers are sponsoring traditional Three-Year Retreats where an average of ten men and ten women spend three years following a strict traditional regime of practice and study, with emphasis on the former. A qualified and experienced lama leads each of these retreats.

Finally, I want to add a personal note. These days, the subject of titles and relative rank has been much discussed. In regard to Kalu Rinpoche, we commonly see the title "Venerable" before his name. However, the reader will note that I have used "His Eminence" throughout this book, a fact which springs from my absolute devotion and respect, as well as my conviction that he has attained complete enlightenment. A well-known spiritual leader and disciple of His Eminence Kalu Rinpoche, Yogi Chen, always uses "His Holiness" when referring to Kalu Rinpoche. I respect that, since his devotion is known to be beyond reproach. It is hoped the reader will give me the same consideration. If this explanation is not satisfactory, the reader is invited to raise the matter with me personally.

I, the devoted student, am always saved by the blessings of Vajradhara.

Lama Lodö
San Francisco

CHAPTER ONE

THE THREE YANAS

This is a very auspicious occasion; it is very fortunate that we could come together for this program of teachings and empowerments. This is due to the kindness of Lama Lodö. All of you who are students and patrons of the dharma, due to your previous karmic connections with this lineage, have come together in this isolated, beautiful place. It is due to this activity on the part of all of you, the support and effort that all of you have shown, that the KDK Center in San Francisco has come together, and likewise, the retreat center here in Oregon. We all have a wonderful opportunity in being here.

First, let us examine the three yanas. They can be viewed in two ways, following two classifications of Buddhist teachings. The more general or common way to view the three yanas is as the Shravaka, the Pratyekabuddha, and the Bodhisattva. The first two beings pertain to the Hinayana level, the third to the Mahayana. Another way of looking at the three yanas is from the point of view of our individual practice. The outer element, our particular lifestyle, pertains to Hinayana individual liberation vows. The inner motivation of our practice is the Bodhisattva attitude of the Mahayana. The secret or hidden aspect of our practice is the experience that we develop through tantric practice, through Vajrayana techniques and our samaya or commitment to that practice.

All three of these yanas, regardless of the particular classification we are using, are the authentic teachings of Lord Buddha Shakyamuni; all of these are part and parcel of the Buddhadharma, the only difference being that while each of these yanas or levels of practice can bring the practitioner to the attainment of complete enlightenment, there is a difference in regard to the time scale in which this happens. Some paths require far longer periods of time for the individual to develop and purify to the attainment of complete enlightenment and other paths are very rapid, comparatively speaking.

There is also a difference with regard to the ability of the practitioner of any one of these yanas or levels of practice to be effective in helping others as well. In some cases, the particular approach that is being used will have greater ability to benefit others as well as oneself through spiritual practice. In the lowest level of the Hinayana path, that of the Shravaka, one who hears the teaching will practice accordingly on that level of the Hinayana. The approach in meditation is to reduce the mind to a momentary state of consciousness which is perceived to be empty, being no thing in itself. So there is partial realization of shunyata at this point. An individual on this level can come to the realization of one aspect of egolessness, that of the individual self, the mind—which is normally taken to be something solid and existent and real, in and of itself. The mind is perceived to be intangible, empty, without any limiting or defining characteristics. However, this realization does not carry through to a point where the practitioner of the Shravaka path can experience the egolessness of all phenomena. Instead, there is the egolessness of the individual, the individual mind or consciousness which is perceived. So there is a fifty percent realization of shunyata. This is the arrival at the halfway point in the possibility for the experience of emptiness or shunyata and it is the highest point that this particular path can take.

Due to our present lack of the experience of this emptiness of mind, we are subject to a great deal of emotional conflict as well as thoughts and ideas which are continually agitating the mind. These, from the point of view of the Hinayana path, are recognized to be something negative, or at least not productive of anything but suffering and confusion. At this point, the approach to the thoughts and emotions of the mind is quite ruthless. One cuts off or arrests this emotional and mental turbulence of the mind, in an attempt to cut off or arrest the origin of suffering and confusion.

This approach also extends to our physical bodies and environments, the world in which we exist. The Hinayanist lives in a mechanistic universe composed of elements which have the potential to be harmful to the physical organism. Earth, air, fire, and water—all of these can be the source of suffering. Also, the relationship to the human body, the physical body, is to regard it as one very basic cause of ego clinging and fixation on the self, which is the primary cause of continued existence in the cycle of rebirth. So the approach is to cut through any fascination with or attachment to the human body, by viewing it as composed of any number of different impure substances. This is accomplished through an analytical process in meditation which dissects the body, as it were, viewing it as flesh and blood, bones and marrow, feces and urine, lymph and internal organs and so forth. The thirty-two impure substances of the body, taken out of context, are unappealing, so by analyzing the body in this way, one is attempting to cut off or arrest any fascination with or clinging to the physical body, regarding it rather as one of the principal bonds or chains keeping the mind caught in the cycle of rebirth. This approach also applies to all the sensory experiences we have through sight, sound, taste, smell, touch, and so forth; all of these are regarded as sources of attachment. We attempt to pull ourselves as far away from any kind of sensory stimulation and attachment as possible, and instead focus the mind inward to develop an awareness of a momentary state of consciousness, which is the key to a partial realization of the emptiness of mind and all experience. In the case of the Shravaka, one realizes the emptiness of the mind without carrying that through to understanding the emptiness or egolessness of all phenomena. Even with this partial realization, however, there comes a release from personal suffering. This is the state of being an Arhat.

The term Arhat, *drachompa* (dgra.bcom.pa) in Tibetan, literally means "one who has conquered the enemy." From the point of view of this yana, this particular vehicle of practice, the thoughts and emotions which contribute to and reinforce our ego clinging are the enemies; they are the foes we are battling since they are blocking our attainment of enlightenment. The practitioner has risen above the limitations that are imposed by conceptual thought and emotions, by placing the mind in this empty state of momentary awareness.

This produces the absence of suffering. The personal experience of an Arhat is total freedom from or transcendence of personal suffering, but the state is a relatively static one. The mind simply remains poised in this state of empty awareness for what may amount to thousands of kalpas, an infinitely long time. One is free of the need to take rebirth again and suffer according to the dictates of karmic tendencies, but totally ineffectual in dealing with the welfare of others. It is a completely neutral or static state of awareness.

At some point, the Arhat will be roused from this state of stagnant partial awareness by a visionary experience of a light being empowered by Buddhas or Bodhisattvas, and will be encouraged to rise above the limitations of the partial realization of emptiness to embark on the Mahayana path. The Arhat will come into contact with a Buddha or Bodhisattva who can transmit the teachings of the Mahayana path and the Arhat will embark on that path, being capable of developing the ability to benefit others and of attaining further realization. The Arhat's path is now identical with the ordinary Mahayana path because the Arhat will have to go through that stage to attain to complete enlightenment.

The intermediate path or yana is that of the Pratyekabuddha, the so-called Self Buddha or Self-made Buddha. For someone who is following this particular approach, the partial experience of emptiness is somewhat extended. The resultant state of awareness is very similar to that of an Arhat, but the particular path which is followed to attain to that state of realization differs. On this level there is emphasis on the twelve *nidanas*, the twelve links of interdependent causality, which form a cycle beginning with fundamental ignorance and following through to birth, old age and death. The process in meditation is one of examining these twelve nidanas from beginning to end and then examining them in reverse order to discover the key to unlocking the whole cycle, which results in the experience of not only the egolessness of the self or individual mind, but also a partial realization of the egolessness of phenomena. Phenomena are no longer taken to be existent in and of themselves but are perceived to be composed of monads or atomic particles to which they are reduced in meditation. However, the final step of realizing the egolessness of the particles is not made. There is a reduction of all phenomena to their subatomic structure but this is still taken to be something ultimately real in and of itself, so there is a partial realization of the egolessness of all phenomena. Thus the Pratyekabuddha can attain to a state which is similar to that of an Arhat in that it is the experience of egolessness of the individual, and also can partially attain a realization of the egolessness of phenomena.

However, while again this entails a personal experience of liberation from suffering, it does not constitute complete enlightenment and it does not constitute a particularly effective state to work for the benefit of others. It is possible for someone who is practicing on this level of dharma to inspire faith in others through the demonstration of miracles such as flying in the sky or manifesting as various elements such as a ball of fire or pool of water. These miraculous powers arise spontaneously from their realizations; they inspire faith in people and plant seeds in them that will result in future rebirths among gods or humans in contact with the teachings. It is therefore beneficial, but there is no ability to actually teach. In fact, this is something noteworthy about the Pratyekabuddha path. The experience of enlightenment is kept to oneself and is not something that is possible to communicate to others; one lacks the effectiveness somehow. Eventually of course, to attain complete enlightenment, the Pratyekabuddha would, as an Arhat does, have to make contact with the Mahayana and follow this particular path through to complete enlightenment; the ability to benefit others would begin to grow in the context of Mahayana practice.

When we consider figures in the lineage of the early spread of the Buddhadharma, such as the seven generations of teachers who followed after the Buddha's passing (the Buddha's Parinirvana), the sixteen Arhats or sixteen Elders of the early Buddhist church, or Shariputra and Maudgalyayana who were the two main students of Buddha, these are individuals who are generally considered to be models of Hinayana practice and individuals who attained the state of an Arhat's realization. However, ultimately speaking, these were very advanced Bodhisattvas manifesting in a particular form as Hinayana individuals, exemplifying this particular model of spiritual practice for the benefit of those people who find it easier to relate to this kind of model. The awareness behind that expression was really much more advanced, much more profound than one might assume, looking at the surface and taking these simply to be Arhats (very advanced, very adept spiritual practitioners but limited in their realization). In fact, it would seem that there was far greater realization and experience behind that which was expressing itself in the choice to manifest in a form which beings at that time and in those circumstances found beneficial.

One model of this Hinayana approach was an individual named Kashyapa who received a particularly significant transmission from the Buddha and functioned as one of the first lineage holders after the

Buddha. He is one of the seven generations of teachers who fulfilled the same function as the Buddha, being the central lineage holders after his Parinirvana. This individual Kashyapa was a married house-holder at one time and he and his wife both practiced the Vedic system of religion under a sage of that tradition. At a certain point both husband and wife became filled with disgust at further involvement in samsara, seeing nothing but suffering and confusion and pain arising from their continued involvement in the cycle of rebirth. Both of them developed a very strong renunciation and a desire to liberate themselves, so they adopted a very strict lifestyle. Although they were married, they adopted a celibate lifestyle and made a vow between themselves that they would have no physical contact nor any sexual activity. They would live as though they were ordained individuals and would refrain from any physical contact, even touching hands.

Once they were on a journey and they lay down to go to sleep under a tree. While Kashyapa was asleep, his wife woke up and saw a poisonous snake coming out of the bushes toward them, and her first thought was to wake him up. But so strong was her commitment to their vow that she felt she shouldn't touch him, even under these circumstances; she took a fly whisk and flapped it at him to wake him up. When he awoke, he thought she had touched him, and he said, "Why have you broken our vow? We can't break our vows; we must stick to them." And she said, "There was a poisonous snake coming and I thought I should wake you up." Kashyapa replied, "It doesn't matter if it bites me. The important thing is to keep the precepts."

That austere approach to life led them to decide that living in the same house was too distracting, so they decided to part ways. Kashyapa went in one direction and his wife went off in the other, to seek their own paths as best they could.

Kashyapa wandered until he came to the particular region in central India where the Buddha was teaching at that time. He met the Buddha and accepted the Buddha as his spiritual teacher. And after taking refuge in the Buddha, he received teachings and began to practice, and eventually attained the realization of an Arhat. It was his strict dedication to that particular approach that allowed him to attain this state of realization, and gave him the sensitivity and development to be able to carry on the Buddha's teachings as one of the main lineage holders.

Kashyapa is a model of Hinayana practice, abandoning worldly concerns to dedicate energy to an austere spiritual practice. This brings us to the Mahayana, which is considered the superior vehicle for a number of reasons. To begin with, the motivation which is necessary to embark on the practice of the Mahayana is an altruistic one: We are taking part in this spiritual activity not simply for our own benefit, but to benefit others. This attitude is something which we need to bring to the Mahayana first and foremost, and is one distinction between the Hinayana and Mahayana. From the very beginning, the keynote is an altruistic one, and that requires commitment. This is not just flashes of altruism, but requires a stable altruistic base upon which to work in order for the practice to be worthy of the title Mahayana. So it is the superior vehicle because of its superior level of motivation.

The results of meditation are also different. We not only realize the emptiness of mind, self and mind having no tangibility whatsoever, but we also carry this through to all experience, all phenomena, as merely manifestations of this empty mind and equally intangible. This is why in the Prajnaparamita literature such as the *Heart Sutra* we find references such as, "There are no eyes, there is no nose, there are no ears, there is no tongue, there is no body, there is no form, there is no sound, there is no smell, there is no taste, there is no touch...." The Prajnaparamita teachings speak of eighteen different aspects of shunyata, covering all phenomena as well as the mind. Through this kind of practice, one arrives not only at the experience of the egolessness of the self or the individual but also the egolessness of all phenomena, the complete experience of shunyata, and therefore there is a difference as to the level of possible accomplishment which merits this term Mahayana—superior vehicle—being used.

There is also a difference on the level of behavior, the way that our meditation manifests in our activities. Because there is an altruistic basis in the Mahayana, the emphasis is on being able to benefit others through what we personally experience in our spiritual practice. Rather than it being a strictly personal experience, the practice and its benefits are something to be shared and spread to others. So the approach to one's practical work in the world is different. For example, in the Mahayana, morality and ethics, moral discipline, is considered to have three different aspects. The first is the narrow sense of the word morality, that is, avoiding negative actions, cutting off or abandoning actions which send one in harmful directions. The second aspect is a kind of morality which consolidates and brings together positive qualities. And the third kind of morality is working for the benefit of other beings, which constitutes in itself a form of moral discipline and ethics.

Now, the first category, the prohibitive side of morality, of actually cutting off or abandoning activities which one feels are harmful to us in terms of our spiritual practice, harmful to ourselves or others—this is something which is common to all three yanas, to the Shravaka, Pratyekabuddha and Bodhisattva paths. The common emphasis in all three is a morality which judges certain activities to be harmful from the point of view of our spiritual development and from the point of view of our ability to help others. Therefore these activities are cut off.

The second aspect of morality and ethics, the encouragement of positive qualities, the use of our faculties in positive ways, is something which is present on the Hinayana level of a Shravaka or Pratyekabuddha in a limited or partial way. What is present in the Hinayana is a sense that controlling our physical actions, developing a correct meditational posture and simplifying our lifestyle so that our physical activities are restricted, encourages positive and moral use of our physical being. Keeping silent and controlling our speech to use it only for positive purposes channels the energy of our speech into a positive direction. A positive moral step is made through the mind being clear of emotional confusion and discursive thought, and letting the mind rest one-pointedly in a state of bare awareness.

However it is only in the Mahayana that we find a really full-blown approach to this second aspect of morality and ethics. There is an emphasis in the Mahayana and particularly in the Vajrayana on many skillful means of using the body, speech and mind in positive ways. Practices such as prostrations, circumambulation of stupas and temples, and the offering of a mandala involving the use of a plate and rice, are physical processes. The recitation of prayers, mantras, texts and sutras are a means of developing verbal merit and verbal virtue. The various methods in meditation to develop faith, to develop compassion, to develop the experience of emptiness in the mind, are associated with a person's individual progress toward enlightenment. These form the second aspect of morality to its fullest extent, and while they are present to some degree in the Hinayana level, it is only in the Mahayana level that we find full expression of this aspect of morality and ethics.

The third aspect of morality, that of working for the benefit of others, is not significantly present on the level of a Shravaka, which remains a purely personal experience and approach in spiritual development. For a Pratyekabuddha, there is some limited ability to manifest miracles or exert some kind of spiritual influence over others, but it is really only on the Mahayana path of the Bodhisattva that one finds specific and explicit references to such practices as the Six Paramitas, which are the means by which a practitioner of the Mahayana expresses commitment to spiritual practice in a way which is beneficial to others. This is not only something which is implied, but is explicitly stated and encouraged in the Mahayana and therefore, of course, in the practice of the Vajrayana as an extension of the superior vehicle. For example, a simple act like eating a meal in a Mahayana context becomes imbued with spiritual significance . As practitioners of the Mahayana, we offer the food to our spiritual teachers and Three Jewels, following which we partake of it; the meal ends with our dedication of the virtue and merit of the offerings and of all practice for the benefit of all beings. This is particularly the case with a meal being offered for the benefit of a patron or sponsor of a meal, but there is always this idea of the sharing of the merit at any meal we eat.

The Vajrayana or tantric approach places even more significance on a simple situation like eating a meal. There is a process known as the inner *ganachakra*, or inner *vajra* feast, in which we meditate the transformation of the food we are eating into a nectar of awareness which we imbibe, identifying ourselves with our *yidam*. We meditate ourselves in the form of the divinity and hold to what is termed the divine pride, the complete identification of ourselves with the divinity. We visualize our guru in the throat chakra, our other meditational divinities in the heart chakra, and the dakinis and dharma protectors of the lineage in the navel chakra. All of the mandalas of the Three Roots are fed or receive offerings by this taking in of the nectar of awareness that the food represents. Through this process of meditation, the whole context of eating a meal becomes charged with a far more profound and beneficial significance, and the means of developing our merit and deepening our awareness by this kind of approach are quite incredible. The dedication of merit and virtue occurs at the end of the meal.

The Vajrayana makes use of any aspect of experience. There is even a technique in the Vajrayana carried out in the act of urinating. We meditate ourselves in the form of Chenrezig (sPyan.ras.gzigs) known as Kasarpani. We meditate that the flow of urine from our body is a flow of nectar. The nectar is that of awareness being shared with the *pretas* and other beings that are not fortunate enough to have direct contact with the teachings. We are attempting through this process to establish some connection through a simple biological act. From the point of view of the Vajrayana this can be imbued with a very profound significance.

In the West, people are not familiar with such an approach, but in Tibet, it was not uncommon for people to make use of these kinds of techniques for even the most ordinary act. For instance, in lighting a fire in the morning to brew a cup of tea, the tantric practitioner would visualize the fire as Vajrasattva, and the fuel as the obscurations and negativities of ourselves and all beings being purified. The practitioner would recite the Vajrasattva mantra while the fire was fed.

For someone who is a practitioner of the Mahayana and Vajrayana and understands the blending of general Mahayana motivation and the specific techniques of the Vajrayana, there is no act that remains meaningless. Each and every act in our daily activity can become a virtuous and spiritually charged situation. As a matter of fact, we are involved with all three yanas. Our personal effort is to develop a lifestyle that is harmless to others, to avoid killing, stealing and so forth. This is an expression of the Hinayana element of our practice. The development of our faith and devotion to the Three Jewels of Buddha, Dharma and Sangha; and the Three Roots of guru, meditational divinities and dharma protectors; our prayers and supplications to these sources of refuge; our prayers and supplications to our guru; the prayers or hymns of praise to our yidam; mandala offerings and prostrations that exist for purifying ourselves and developing our merit and awareness are in the context of the Mahayana or Vajrayana, depending upon the particular technique that is being used.

In this level of practice our loving kindness and compassion toward other beings becomes paramount. Recognizing other beings as our parents due to karmic connections from previous existences supports this. Our awareness of the essentially positive nature of that past connection and our awareness of the ignorance that now creates disharmony, confusion and separation between beings is the basis from which to develop compassion in the Mahayana context. The Mahayana approach also emphasizes our efforts to be as beneficial as possible to others in any situation; even when we are not physically able to be helpful, our compassion and loving kindness and positive aspirations on behalf of other beings are a very significant factor. Any attempt to develop altruism in ourselves and any attempt to manifest this in physical activity or aspirations to benefit others is extremely important for our involvement in the Mahayana in general and the Vajrayana in particular.

Throughout an infinite process of rebirth after rebirth, the single common denominator has been the concept of the "I" the self, the mind, as something real and solid and individual in and of itself. It is this concept which gives rise to the cycle of rebirth in the first place and continues to fuel it. Any attempt to attain complete enlightenment is an attempt to transcend the limitations of that fixation on the self or ego. That is why the meditation of Chenrezig is so important. In that meditation, which is Mahayana in spirit but Vajrayana in technique, there is the attempt not only to foster positive qualities such as loving kindness and compassion for others; but there is also the attempt to eliminate this fixation on the ego. We shift the focus from the self to the form of the divinity as a step toward the final transcendence of all fixation; the practitioner will transcend the limitation of ego and break through into the experience of true egolessness, the ultimate nature of mind itself. The recitation of the mantra *OM MANI PADME HUNG*, which is one of the single most beneficial mantras of the tantric path, and our use of the visualization in states of meditative absorption, are very important from the point of view of liberating the mind from the necessity to experience according to the dictates of ego, to experience things as *real*.

There are three aspects to the Mahayana and Vajrayana, the view with which we go about the practice; the specific technique of meditation through which we maintain and develop that view; and the particular deportment or activity that is encouraged in the way we express our realization or experience in daily activity. On the Mahayana and Vajrayana level, the correct view is nothing less than the direct experience of the ultimate nature of mind itself; only at that level can we say that someone has completely realized the view of the superior vehicle. As long as there is only a partial realization, we are speaking of only a partial understanding of the view.

People often say that there seems to be a significant difference between Eastern world view and Western world view. Actually, there seems to be a greater difference between a secular world view and a spiritual world view. Whether we come from an Eastern culture or a Western culture, if we do not understand the concept of karma, we have a secular world view. Whether we are Eastern or Western is not going to make any difference that is going to benefit us on any ultimate level. Western people for the most part, for example, have a great deal of doubt about the nature of mind—whether mind exists or not in any ultimate sense. Westerners also seem to have doubt about the concept of future or previous existences and about the continuity of mind from one existence to another. There is a tendency to focus merely on this plane, on this life, as the given, the ultimate reality, and to work from there. Now people in the East are no different if they have not received spiritual training and have not developed themselves through the practice of dharma. They see things very much the same way. So what we are speaking about rather than the differences between East and West are the differences between the worldly and the transcendent or spiritual. Whether we come from the East or the West, we can receive very great benefit from developing a spiritual world view which sees beyond the limitations of dimensions.

I will describe the nature of mind briefly by saying that the mind is essentially empty but luminous in nature, in terms of its potential or ability to know, and unimpeded and dynamic in its manifestations as cognition or awareness. Now, this is something we have to validate for ourselves once we have grasped these ideas. We have to validate it through our own direct experience. We have to sit down and look for the mind. Is there something there? Ultimately, of course, the search is going to be fruitless. We are not going to find the mind, because there is no thing that is the mind. Nevertheless we have to go through this process of sitting down and examining the mind and examining our experience to see what is really going on. What, if anything, is happening? It is only through this kind of approach that we come to some significant understanding; perhaps it is not complete enlightenment, but at least we have a glimpse.

Our actual approach is not so much looking for the mind as allowing the mind to relax, allowing the mind to experience its true nature. It is not as though we were not looking at all, because there is this alertness or awareness to the mind, there is this spark of intelligent awareness which should not be lost if the meditation is to be effective. Slowly we come to understand more about the nature of mind, the immortality of mind, the deathlessness of mind in and of itself, rather than the particular projections of the mind such as the physical body. With the understanding of continuity from one life to another, we can still be caught in a relative framework, the apparent solidity of the physical body, for example, and can make very good use of it. Given that the mind will go on beyond the death of the physical body and experience some other state, then it seems only sensible that if we are concerned about happiness and fulfillment in this life, we are going to be concerned about the same things in future existences. We are going to want to assure that the continued experience of the mind is as happy and as fulfilled and as beneficial as possible. This gives us a basis for moral choices in our present life, a basis upon which to make a choice between whether an action is virtuous or non-virtuous, whether it is helpful or harmful.

By appreciating the emptiness of mind, we begin to appreciate the emptiness of all phenomena, of all experiences as merely arising from the mind. What we tend to do right now with an ordinary worldly outlook is to take this body, this life, this state of existence as ultimate reality. We think of everything as real and solid in and of itself and we go about life in that way. However, as we meditate, we begin to understand the relative reality and non-reality of everything that we experience. The physical body came into being as a result of certain karmic tendencies maturing in the individual consciousness, giving rise to this temporary experience of something as solid as the physical body. But it ages, it dies, it decomposes; it is not something eternal.

Similarly, everything that we experience now lacks any kind of ultimate reality, ultimate stability, because the quality of the projections that arise from mind is continual impermanence, change and flux, where nothing remains the same because there is nothing to remain the same. Once we begin to experience that, we see the illusory or dreamlike nature of all experience, all phenomena. The physical body of the universe is merely temporary appearances coming together as a result of various causes and conditions acting together in certain ways, but certainly nothing to which we could ever ascribe any ultimate independent reality.

There is a collective aspect to this karmic process because we share certain elements of our experience. We are all human beings in the same realm of experience. We see the same physical environment and experience that same physical environment of rocks and trees and rivers and so forth. All of this is due to the fact that we share a certain common karma and thus share a relatively coherent view of the universe. However, we all have individual experiences which are not shared with others. Some people are happy while other people are unhappy. Some people are rich while other people are poor. Some people are healthy while others are unhealthy. These individual aspects of karma remain purely personal experiences because they are the result of tendencies that were developed on an individual level.

What we experience now is, ultimately speaking, an illusion very much like a dream. When we go to sleep and have a dream, we experience the dream as something real. There are forms we see. There are sounds we hear. There are things we interact with in a dream which give it a real internal logic. We wake up and the dream is gone and nobody would ascribe any reality to that dream. What we experience now in both its collective and its individual aspects has that same quality of a dream because eventually when we die, we leave it all behind and the entire experience that was this life disappears just as a dream disappears when we awaken.

This impermanence is something which also expresses itself on the level of our individual consciousness, in the emotions of passion, aggression, stupidity, pride, jealousy and greed which continually arise in the mind. None of those can be considered ultimately real. There is continual change and instability in the mind, continual arising and breaking down of emotional patterns, thoughts and concepts. However, let us take heart, because if these things were real in and of themselves, we would have no room to move in the situation. Because none of these thoughts or emotions or circumstances are real in and of themselves, we can work with them. Through the practice of dharma we can come to change the way in which we experience things because, given that they have no ultimate reality in and of themselves, there is no reason for these aspects of experience to dominate us. We are perfectly able, with the practice of dharma, to know the benefit that comes from being able to take control over our own experience.

We can see, in the way the world is structured around us, that things are always moving in cycles and nothing is stable. Take water as an example. We see a continual flow of rivers and streams into the oceans of the world and the oceans never seem to overflow because the water is redirected by means of water coming up from under the earth; there is a seemingly unlimited supply of water coming from under the earth which doesn't exhaust itself, no matter how much water flows up in springs and geysers and so forth. There is no fixed or solid nature to any of the elements in this situation, but continual impermanence, a continual flux and flow.

This inexhaustible change and impermanence is something that we see on an individual level as well. There seems to be no end to the thoughts and emotions that we can come up with in our minds; there seems to be no end to the words that we can come up with to speak. These are not things which are fixed or limited in any way, but exhibit the kind of inexhaustibility which derives from their fundamental impermanence and fundamental lack of ultimate reality.

Why do we pursue such an investigation? It gives us a greater perspective so that we are not so attached to this life, this particular reality, this particular physical body, this particular self. The benefit that we experience through loosening the bonds of clinging to things as solid and real is that the practice of any kind of meditation and any kind of mental discipline becomes far easier and far more effective. Also, the personal experience of suffering and conflict diminishes as this naive clinging to things as ultimately real begins to dissipate. This is not to say that we are entirely free from or should not respect the relativistic patterns that we are caught up in, because the karmic process is something that remains perfectly valid and infallible. In fact, until our realization allows us to transcend the limitations of karmic process, our physical, verbal and mental efforts to develop and purify ourselves are very important. Thus we can, while still working within a relative framework, control it to a certain extent, so that our own experience of that process is as positive as possible. Then the mind continues from happiness to greater happiness and from fulfillment to greater fulfillment because of our skillful use of and respect of the limitations of karma.

QUESTIONS

There seems to be an implication that the Hinayana path is limited whereas the Vajrayana path is the complete one. Have there been controversies or conflicts about this?

We have no reliable sources about the present situation, but we can refer to the historical development of Buddhism to give us an example of the problems that are sometimes encountered when different levels of teaching are presented. The early spread of Buddhism was largely Hinayana in flavor; the model for spiritual practice tended to be that of the monk and the Arhat. When the Buddha began to teach about shunyata and the emptiness of all phenomena, it is reported that people at his teachings would plug their ears rather than hear that teaching because it threatened their world view too much. It was too profound and they simply could not accept it, so they would refuse to hear it.

It doesn't seem to me that there needs to be a lot of conflict about this in America. You might be a farmer and you do your farming well. This is the way you make your livelihood and this is the way you like to work; you think farming is a perfectly good vocation. You know that there are airplane pilots and cab drivers and physicians and lawyers and so forth, but you're a farmer. They can do what they want and you do what you want. So, it would seem that in the area of spiritual practice that this would be a fairly healthy attitude. Everybody can know what everybody else is doing but it is what you do that is important. If you are doing it well and you are doing what you feel is the best for you, then that is probably the single most constructive approach you can have. You have made your own decision; there need not be any conflict.

The Tibetan tradition does encompass all three yanas. There is a monastic tradition in Tibetan Buddhism. People wear robes and there is emphasis on moral discipline and the individual liberation vows; this is perfectly in accord with the Hinayana path. There is also a very strong emphasis on bodhicitta and the bodhisattva vow and bodhisattva activity, which is perfectly in accord with the Mahayana. There is also a very rich tradition of tantra, the empowerments and teachings for Vajrayana and the different techniques of meditation that we can use in Vajrayana for people who are drawn to that. So the point of the Tibetan approach to Buddhism is an attempt to integrate all of these. It is not so much that there is something for everybody and you pick and choose among them, but that the whole integrates all of the parts.

Will you talk about memory, not simply short-term but also that of previous lifetimes? What is the relationship between mind and body? Is anything stored in the body? Is the Buddha's consciousness more than a blank state? Does it involve thought and memory and mental processes rather than just being blank?

The reason why memory is possible at all, even in a very limited way, is because the nature of mind is empty, clear and unimpeded. Because the mind is empty and no thing in and of itself, it can and does pervade every aspect of experience, regardless of whether we realize that consciously or not. Because it has the potential to experience anything whether we realize it or not, and because it has the dynamic manifestation of awareness which can experience anything, the mind has the ability to recall events which occurred in previous times. The mind is not actually limited to the present moment, though we feel that it is.

As we develop an experience of the pervasive empty nature of mind, which is not any different from the mind that we experience at this moment, the scope of it begins to expand. Our memory begins to increase; our ability to see into the future as well as the past begins to increase. This is something that is noted in the process of meditation; we become aware of more in all directions, not just linearly into the past. The experience of a fully enlightened Buddha, far from being a blank state, is an enhancing of what we now experience At the level of Buddha-consciousness, there is even greater awareness than we presently have and that is why we can speak of omniscience, literally being aware of everything.

On a very pragmatic level, there are signs that this begins to happen, that the mind begins to increase its scope, and that is why it is said that a first-level Bodhisattva not only sees with the eyes but hears with the eyes, tastes with the eyes, touches and feels with the eyes, smells with the eyes, and thinks with the eyes. A particular avenue of consciousness can operate in other ways because the mind begins to expand and increase its ability to express itself.

This does not preclude that on a relativistic level, when we are still caught up in a vast illusionary scheme of things, certain circumstances can contribute to situations happening in certain ways. The idea, for example, of certain organs being the seat of certain emotions, is perfectly acceptable within a relative framework, but there is no need to ascribe any ultimate reality to it. Within a particular situation there may be a configuration of the psycho-physical structure of the organism that indicates a link between organ and emotion, for example, the liver and anger or the heart and desire, but that does not mean that on any ultimate level we would say that it is because of the organ that any particular emotion arises.

We can take the case of a lower form of life like an invertebrate, such as a leech or a bloodsucker. These are very common in the East and some of them get quite large. They slide along the floor of the forest and as soon as they get near a warm-blooded creature, they attach themselves to it and start drinking the blood. If you dissect one of those things you do not find any organ systems at all. There is really little there except a sheaf of tissue that can absorb blood, but it has got a consciousness. It does not have a skeletal structure. It does not have any well-developed circulatory system or respiratory system or digestive system, but it still has emotions. It can still feel pleasure and pain. It can still feel desire and frustration. There is consciousness on that level even though the particular physical envelope is very primitive when compared with something like the human organism.

Why do the Buddhas wait thousands of years to send light to the Arhats?

The Buddhas are sending light to the Arhats at all times. However the Arhats are not clear enough to sense it until they have been in a state of awareness for much time.

CHAPTER TWO

ORDINARY PRELIMINARY PRACTICES

The preliminary practices are the approach to the practice of dharma. The Tibetan term *Ngöndro* (sngon.'gro), which is used to describe this phase of practice, literally means "something that goes before, something which precedes." This is rather like the example of wanting to drive a car. First you must have a road on which to drive; if you haven't prepared that surface, then there is no way to drive the car. The idea of Ngöndro as a preliminary or foundation practice is to prepare that road for one's practice of dharma to continue in a certain direction. These preliminary practices can be considered to be of two kinds. The first is the common or ordinary kind of preliminary and the second is the special or particular kind of preliminary practice.

The ordinary preliminaries are the contemplation that we term "the four thoughts which turn the mind." They turn it away from involvement in samsara and toward the practice of dharma. It is a solid understanding and appreciation of these four thoughts, these four contemplations, that arouse in the mind a sincere commitment to the practice of dharma. Without having understood these preliminary considerations one cannot generate sufficient motivation and sufficient sincerity to carry through with one's practice of the dharma. Because this is the case, these four thoughts are not particular to any one school of Buddhism, but common to all of them, so they are called the common or ordinary preliminaries. We can even find elements of them in other religions too. If we examine the iconography of Christian painting, we find the symbolism of skulls and skeletons as the symbols of mortality and impermanence. These concepts pervade the religious and spiritual systems of the world, because there is this common or fundamental quality to them.

The first thought that turns the mind toward the dharma is an appreciation of the precious human existence. The term used in Tibetan to describe this state of existence is *dal-jor* (dal.'byor), which literally means "a freedom or opportunity difficult to come by." This phrase denotes that the precious human existence provides us with certain opportunities and freedoms that allow spiritual practice to take place. The term *dal* indicates a sense of leisure or a sense of freedom from restriction. The term *jor* has the sense of an opportunity or something very positive that one has in abundance so that one is able to profit from it.

In the precious human existence, the freedom in this state is the freedom of not having taken rebirth in the eight states of fettered existence where one lacks the opportunity to practice dharma. The first three fettered states are rebirths in the three lower realms of existence—the hell realms, the preta realms, and the animal realms. The fourth is rebirth in the higher realms of the gods and the demi-gods. Though these last two are superior states of rebirth in samsara, they do not provide one with spiritual opportunity but merely the experience of pleasure.

The other four of the eight fettered states concern the human realm. These are being born in a land where there is no dharma; being born as a person whose nature does not appreciate or respect spiritual teachings, even though one may be surrounded by them; being born in an era, or kalpa, when Buddhas do not appear; and being born with some impairment of one's faculties which prevents one from being able to understand or receive teachings.

In not having been born into these eight states of hindered or fettered existence, one is enjoying a considerable state of freedom as a human being. For example, in the hell realms, the minds of the beings suffer so intensely from the continual anguish of extreme heat or extreme cold that the mind is totally absorbed in this experience of agony; there is no chance that the mind can direct itself toward anything like spiritual practice. The same absorption occurs in the preta realms. Because these beings suffer from hunger, thirst and a sense of deprivation, and because there is continual preoccupation of the mind in experiencing this intense suffering, the mind cannot come into contact with or appreciate spiritual teachings.

The same can be said of the animal realm, though the particular limiting factor there is the incredible stupidity in the minds of animals, in that they are not sufficiently developed intellectually to come into contact with a teacher and receive spiritual teachings and implement them in their lives. In fact there is no opportunity for an animal to encounter a Buddha or Bodhisattva spiritual teacher, not because these teachers do not try to manifest in these realms, but the beings in those realms lack sensitivity due to their karmic obscurations. So these first three fettered or hindered states are the three lower realms of existence in the cycle of rebirth and for the various reasons just mentioned, these states of existence do not provide beings in these realms with the opportunity to develop themselves through the practice of dharma.

The next realm of fettered existence that the texts speak of is that of the gods. Here we are speaking of beings that inhabit the three realms of samsara: the desire realm, the form realm, and the formless realm of existence. The particular catch of the desire realm gods' existence is dissipation and distraction due to the sensual pleasure that those beings experience as a result of their conventional merit. It may be possible for such a being to come into contact initially with the teachings of dharma. They may encounter something as fundamental as the four marks of Buddhadharma which state that everything compounded is subject to impermanence; that everything that is subject to exhaustion creates suffering and frustration; that each and every phenomenon is essentially empty, lacking any real self or ultimate reality; and that nirvana, the transcendence of suffering, is ultimate peace. It may be possible for a being in these desire realms of the gods to understand and appreciate that teaching and think, "You know, I really should do something about this; I really should practice dharma." However, in the next instant, the mind is wandering into some pleasant experience, and it cannot be focused for very long.

In the form realm of existence, the gods are experiencing a kind of samadhi, a trance-like state. This is not an eternal state of enlightenment, since it is subject to exhaustion and degeneration at some point, but a blank state. Therefore, there is not the intellectual comprehension necessary to meet the dharma. In the formless realms the gods are in such a state of nearly nonconceptual consciousness that nothing as structured as spiritual teaching can take place. So, whether we are talking about a god in the desire, form, or formless realms, there is no occasion for that being to come into contact with the teachings of dharma in any significant way.

The next state which is mentioned in the traditional text is that of barbarians, of spiritual barbarism, and there would seem to be many areas in the human realm nowadays where this spiritual barbarism is the case. There may be injunctions against religious practice in a certain area, or it may be that a certain area has not been exposed to the teachings of something like Buddhadharma, so that these spiritual concepts are not part of the common view.

Sixthly, the texts speak of those who have views naturally antagonistic to those of the dharma. Even if they live in a place where the teachings are present and accessible, they reject them. They reject any idea of the continuity of mind from previous existences to future existences; and any idea of causality, the relationship between actions and experience.

The seventh of these eight hindered states is being born in a time in which Buddhas do not appear. During our particular kalpa, from the time this world system we inhabit was formed until its destruction, there will appear a total of one thousand Buddhas, which means that this is an extremely fortunate kalpa. Following this, there will be a period of sixty such kalpas where no Buddha will appear at all. Then there will be one kalpa in which Buddhas will appear, following which there will be seven hundred kalpas in which Buddhas will not appear, following which there will be one in which Buddhas will appear. From one age to another, there is no guarantee that Buddhas will appear. It is an extremely rare occurrence, when seen on a cosmic scale, that Buddhas actually appear in any given age and present the teachings of dharma; or that the word dharma is even present in the language; or that the concept even exists at all.

The eighth kind of hindrance that could be a part of one's existence is some kind of impairment or retardation. This could be a sensory impairment, such as being born blind or deaf, or it could be a mental impairment, such as being born without the intelligence necessary to understand and implement spiritual teachings. Any of these impairments would make one's pursuit of the dharma difficult, if not impossible.

When one has attained a state of human existence free from any of these eight possibilities which would hinder or limit one's ability to receive and implement the teachings, one is enjoying what are termed the eight freedoms associated with the precious human rebirth. Therefore, one has the ability to understand and practice the teachings of dharma. However, even if one were enjoying these eight freedoms, that would not guarantee that one would meet with and practice the teachings; this is what the texts refer to by maintaining that there are also ten opportunities. Five of them come about through others and five of them come about through one's own situation or actions. It is necessary for all of these to be present for one to meet the teachings and actually practice them.

The five opportunities that come about through others are the appearance of a Buddha, the teaching that the Buddha presents, the maintenance and duration of that Buddha's teachings, the following of those teachings by others, and the kindness and support that one is shown by others in one's practice. Now, as we have already mentioned, there are many kalpas in which Buddhas do not appear. In those ages, the first two opportunities would be missing; the teaching would not take place and one could never come into contact with it. In our particular case, the Buddha Shakyamuni appeared in India hundreds of years ago and taught a very extensive and profound cycle of teachings of three yanas, Hinayana, Mahayana and Vajrayana. (This is not something which every Buddha does. Some appear, but do not teach.)

Shakyamuni Buddha having appeared and taught, there occurs a span of time in which his teachings remain present before they gradually disappear. Then there follows quite a long interval before the next Buddha appears, during which there are no teachings at all, though one is still within the context of this age where one thousand Buddhas will appear. We live in a time when the teachings of Shakyamuni Buddha are a living transmission. There are also many people who continue to follow these teachings, providing one with an example, and it is because of their involvement in the teachings that there has been this living transmission.

Finally, there is the kindness and support that others show for one's practice. This is something that is quite important because without support, be it financial or moral, one might have all the intention in the world but be unable to practice. However, in fact, that support is forthcoming from individuals who are impressed by the teachings, impressed by one's interest in and practice of the teachings, and they therefore provide support out of kindness and affection for one as a practitioner.

An example of this last point can be appreciated by looking at the general situation since I first came to America in 1971. There were many people who were interested in practice but they had no support from the culture around them whatsoever. Now, in a very short span of time, we see that increased interest has given a greater sense of support. For example, people are now going into the three-year, three-month retreat program. Some of them are entering without adequate funds to complete that retreat, but we are finding that many people are inspired to support them. This is not something that really could have happened even a short time ago and is an example of affectionate and compassionate support for one's practice by other people. So all of these opportunities that are provided by the actions of others are necessary for anyone to enjoy the precious human existence.

Of course, even though there might be much support and opportunity forthcoming from others, it remains for individuals to provide themselves with opportunities. The five opportunities we are concerned with are having taken a human rebirth, having been born in what is technically termed a central country, having been born with all one's faculties intact, living one's life in such a way that one does not fall into some karmic extreme or cul-de-sac which leads one away from the teachings, and having a basic faith and confidence in the teachings of dharma. These are the five opportunities that are provided from one's own situation.

In the first of these, one has avoided the eight fettered or hindered existences and taken rebirth as a human in this precious state of existence. Next, being born in a central country is interpreted to mean a historical or geographical place such as the areas of India where the Buddha appeared, or it can be any place where the teachings of dharma are present. We find ourselves in that situation, in a country where the teachings of dharma have spread and are spreading; this area has become a central country from the viewpoint of Buddhadharma.

The third concern is that one is born with all of one's senses intact. The fourth point is having lived one's life in a way which has directed one toward rather than away from the dharma. This means that one has not, due to the influence of one's parents or family or friends or one's own inclinations, concerned oneself solely with something extremely mundane; but has continued to maintain some sensitivity for the teachings of dharma. All of this is very important, but there must be this fifth point, which is the basic confidence in and attraction for the teachings of dharma. This is something which we as individuals enjoy in this precious state of rebirth.

When the eight states of freedom and the ten opportunities are complete, then one is speaking about a precious human existence. All of you reading this are now in that kind of human existence. We may feel that there are billions of people in the world so we may be confident that if we die we will probably take a human rebirth, but we do not have any kind of guarantee because of the extreme rarity of the precious human state of existence.

We can consider the rarity of the precious human existence in a number of ways. The Buddha gave certain examples to illustrate and impress the rarity of this occasion upon his listeners. First of all, by considering the karmic cause which results in one taking rebirth in such a fortunate state of existence, one can appreciate its rarity; it is only through a process of moral choice between unskillful, unvirtuous actions and skillful, virtuous actions, that a being establishes a sufficiently positive karma to attain to this kind of precious human rebirth. When one looks at the various forms of life, one can see that the actual number of beings involved in that kind of moral choice, avoiding negative and harmful actions and encouraging in themselves virtuous and positive ones, are very few. Because those who are developing the cause are very few, therefore those who are going to experience the result will be correspondingly few.

Secondly, one can consider the number of beings in various realms. Buddha tried to illustrate this when he compared the number of beings in the hell realm to the number of atoms in the earth, the number of pretas to the grains of sand in all the lakes and oceans and rivers in the world, and the number of animals to the number of drops of rain or flakes of snow that fall. This indicates the enormity, the immensity of the number of beings in those realms, by comparison to which the number of beings in the human realm is very small.

In particular, the number of beings in the human realm enjoying this precious human state of rebirth are extremely rare and the Buddha compared them to the appearance of stars in the daytime. It is possible to see such a thing, but very, very rare; in the same way, it is possible for such a being to have that state of rebirth, but it is very, very rare. The Buddha used a metaphor at one point to illustrate this rarity of the precious human rebirth. He said that if the whole earth were covered with water, and at the bottom of this vast ocean lived a tortoise which was blind and only rose to a random point on the surface of the ocean once in every hundred years, and if on the surface of that ocean there was a yoke made of wood, which was being buffeted about by the wind and waves in a random fashion, how often would the tortoise rise and put its head through the hole in that piece of wood? We cannot rule out the possibility, but obviously it is not going to happen very often. That is the kind of rarity that the precious human rebirth represents.

The first preliminary practice, then, is to recognize and appreciate the precious human state of rebirth and to appreciate its potential. This precious human rebirth offers us incredible opportunity for the practice of dharma and for spiritual development; we cannot expect this opportunity to come again and again. Moreover, life is brief. If we appreciate these things, we will see the need to make use of this precious human state of rebirth and to truly realize the potential of being human while we have the opportunity.

Not to make use of our opportunity would be an incredible waste. It would be like a pauper being presented with a hundred kilos of gold and then sitting there the rest of his life, not knowing what to do with the gold, and dying as poor as ever. It is a wasted opportunity. We have been given that wealth; we have found that wealth in our situation and if we do not do something meaningful with it, then we are wasting something quite incredible. We can do something significant with our spiritual development, we can make moral choices in life, choosing between virtue and nonvirtue, and develop realization and insight. We have the potential to attain complete enlightenment, the ultimate achievement for our own welfare and for helping others as well. Once we have an appreciation of what the human potential provides, we can develop the motivation to actually realize that potential through the practice of dharma.

As humans, we make the naive assumption that things around us are stable, solid, and eternal. The second preliminary practice is to become aware of death, impermanence and change in every aspect of our experience.

This can be considered on a number of levels. We can take a cosmic viewpoint and consider the world system in which we live. It seems so solid now, but ultimately it is going to be destroyed; eventually, there will be a process of dissolution through fire and water and elements breaking up. On a cosmic scale, we can see that nothing is eternal.

One can also examine our annual experience of the changing of the seasons. Spring passes into summer, then autumn into winter in a continual cycle. This is a continual process of change.

Even on a daily basis, nothing is ever stable; nothing is ever constant; nothing remains the same. Everyday one gets up. It is dawn, it is early morning, midmorning, midday, afternoon, evening, nightfall, night. One has a watch; one can sit and look at the watch and see life ticking by second by second. There is relentless change and relentless instability to everything we experience.

And most significantly from one's own point of view, one can consider one's span of life, which is shortening, second by second, minute by minute, hour by hour, day by day. This is a process that cannot be stopped. It is a relentless process of change and impermanence that we experience in everything, including, significantly, our own life.

Everyone who has ever been born in this realm has died; everyone who has been born and is still alive is going to die; everyone in the future who will be born will die. This is the nature of things. Everything that is born is subject to death—and we are no different. In particular, we live in a realm where the span of life is not fixed. People die at all ages. Some children are stillborn; some die in infancy. Some people die in youth or middle age or old age. There is no certainty.

No one of us can say, "I am going to live this long," and guarantee it. We understand the precious potential we have in being human, but we do not know how long that opportunity is going to last. It is something we need to understand so that we can appreciate the necessity of using our precious potential as quickly as possible. Once we have that appreciation, we will find that we have no trouble at all practicing dharma.

The benefits of appreciating the implications of impermanence are something that Milarepa addressed when he said, "It was fear of death that drove me to the mountains, and I meditated so long on death and impermanence that I realized the deathless state of my mind. Now death holds no fears for me."

Sooner or later we are all going to die and the experience of death is a very traumatic one. If we do not utilize this life for the practice of dharma, part of our suffering and pain at the point of death will spring from recognizing our wasted opportunity. We will think to ourselves, "If only I had practiced sooner, if only I had not waited. Now there is no time." When death comes, death comes. There is no way to forestall it and try to make up for the lost time that resulted from one's procrastination. It is now while we do have the opportunity that we need to see the opportunity and make use of it, so that we will have no regrets.

If it were the case that the more we heard about or thought about death and impermanence, the shorter life got, then there would be an argument against mentioning it. But whether or not we think about death, we are going to die; and whether or not we think of the impermanence of things, things are impermanent. At least by being mindful of this, we can develop an awareness that instills the commitment to practice, so that when we do inevitably have to die, we can at least go to death cheerfully. We can feel, "Well, I haven't wasted my life. I've made a good thing of my life and a significant amount of virtue has taken place." We do not have to go to death with regrets.

The third of the common preliminaries is the concept of karma: the causality between actions and experience. This is something so crucial to the understanding of Buddhadharma that the Buddha regarded it as the essence of all of his teachings. At one point the Buddha said, "Once a karmic tendency has been established, it won't exhaust itself in a million kalpas; it won't go away. At a certain point when the conditions come together which require it to emerge, it will ripen; it will mature into experience." Given that there is this infallibility of the karmic process, we must not expect our karma to get lost so that we will not have to account for it.

It is important to understand how the karmic process works, because it is such a crucial and infallible aspect of our own experience. We can examine a few general aspects of the karmic process here. Those who are interested in a more exhaustive description would do well to consult the *Jewel Ornament of Liberation* by Gampopa. Also, in my own small book, *The Writings of Kalu Rinpoche*, there is a reasonably complete though concise treatment of this theme of karma.

To begin with, there is both a collective and an individual aspect to karma. For example, we have all taken rebirth as human beings in this particular realm, so we have a certain element of shared karma. A certain percentage of our experience as human beings in this realm is due to a collective or common kind of karma. However, within that general context, some of us live longer than others; some are happier than others; some are healthier than others. This range, this spectrum of individual human experience is due to the individual aspect of karma. While each individual shares a certain element with every other individual in this realm, there are individual karmic patterns and tendencies which result in individual variations of experience for each person.

There is a story of a certain individual who was born during the lifetime of Shakyamuni Buddha. This young boy was born with a beautiful jewel in his ear. When it was appraised by experts it was found to be worth one million units of the currency of the day—a fabulous jewel. The boy quickly became known as The Million Dollar Ear. At a certain point during his life he came into contact with the Buddha and received teaching from the Buddha and set himself to meditation. He very quickly attained the level of an Arhat, the realized saint of the Hinayana level of practice. Understandably, people were curious about him, due to the remarkable circumstances of his birth and also his very rapid spiritual progress, so they asked the Buddha to explain what the karmic causes of such a rebirth were.

The Buddha explained that an infinitely long time ago there had been a wealthy merchant who had a beautiful earring with a very costly gem in it. In his travels, he had come across some people erecting a stupa or monument to a particular Buddha and he was so inspired by faith that he decided to sponsor the project; he took the beautiful jewel from his ear and gave it to the people who were working on the stupa. The merit that he developed from that sincere act of generosity and faith set up a karmic tendency whereby his mind took rebirth in human and godly states for a long period of time until he was born during the time of Shakyamuni Buddha under these very remarkable circumstances of the jewelled ear. Because of the spiritual connection he had established through faith and appreciation of the stupa, he came into contact with the Buddha. That event created the positive karmic tendency which allowed him to make rapid spiritual progress. We are constantly experiencing the maturation of karmic tendencies which were established in previous lifetimes through our actions.

Also during the lifetime of Lord Buddha, another remarkable occurrence was the experience of a particular woman who, when she was very young, married and conceived her first child. However, she did not give birth to this child after the normal term of pregnancy. Instead she conceived a second child and following a normal term of nine months, gave birth to the second child. During her life she gave birth to ten children and the first fetus that had been conceived but never born remained in her womb all of this time.

When she was in her seventies and had been carrying this first child for sixty years, she was dying. She exacted a promise from her doctor and her family that when she died, the fetus would be delivered by Caesarean section because, she said, "I know the child is still in my womb; I have been pregnant eleven times and given birth to ten children and I know I am still carrying this first fetus in my womb. I want to make sure the child is going to be looked after. I am sure it is still alive; I am sure it has been developing all this time and I want its life to be preserved after I die."

Understandably, this became quite well known and many people gathered when she was dying. The Buddha also became aware of this situation and, with a large number of his followers, he came to the place where the woman was dying. When the doctor pronounced her dead, he performed a Caesarean section and lifted from her womb a living being who was not a baby, but a kind of small dwarfish figure that resembled an old man with white hair. He also lacked teeth. In fact, it looked as though the teeth had formed and then fallen out, for the face was sunken. This wizened little figure was lifted from the womb of the dead woman and the Buddha blessed the child, or rather, old being, and gave it the power of speech. The Buddha said to it, "You seem to be quite old; you are, aren't you?"

The little dwarfish figure replied, "Yes, I am quite old." The name Old One was given to it for want of a better name. The amazing thing was that this human being, this old child, was able to develop intelligence and learn to walk and talk and become a functioning individual; more remarkable than that, it was able to attain Arhatship through the spiritual teaching of the Buddha.

The Buddha explained that this particular karmic situation had begun during the time of the previous Buddha, Sangye Korwajik (Sangs.rgyas.'Khor.ba.'jig). An old and venerable monk who was very developed in his meditation had a young novice as his attendant and their relationship was very harmonious. One day, however, a large festival came to the area and the young monk was eager to go. He went to his teacher and said, "Why don't we both go to this fair?"

The teacher said, "Well, both of us have taken monk's vows. We don't need to go to spectacles. The most important thing for us to do is to sit and meditate and develop ourselves spiritually." He would not give his permission and he himself did not want to go, so the young monk asked permission to go alone. The old monk reiterated that they should be doing their meditation. The novice continued to press for permission to go and the teacher continued to refuse.

Finally, the young monk became furious and started to scold and abuse his guru. He said, "I don't care if you sit and rot in a hole for sixty years; I'm going to the carnival," and he left. He developed such an aversion to his teacher that it established a karmic tendency that eventually ripened as he spent a lifetime in his mother's womb before being born. However, because of the previous positive connections he had had, and the basic virtue he had established in that earlier lifetime, he was able to make contact with the Buddha and make very rapid spiritual progress.

Again during the Buddha's lifetime a monstrous creature appeared in a large open sewer close to the city of Varanasi. This strange creature had eighteen heads and each one resembled the head of a different animal, such as a horse, a monkey and a sheep. A report of this came to the Buddha's ears and he went to see this creature with a large number of people following. As he came to the bank of the foul pool, the creature came to the surface and came toward him and he bestowed his blessing on the creature and said, "Do you remember what it was you did that brought this about?"

The memory of this strange creature stirred and it began to understand what the karmic causes had been which led to its present existence. It began to cry, for in a previous existence it had been a monk who had a particularly foul mouth. He gave his fellow monks very derogatory nicknames, mocking how their faces were formed, such as "pig face" and "monkey face." This karmic tendency eventually became the stream of consciousness and resulted in this very graphic manifestation of negativity. The Buddha blessed the creature and liberated its consciousness from its lower state of existence and the being attained to a higher state of rebirth in the god realms.

Another occurrence during the life of the Buddha concerned an old couple who had lived their lives in a very simple way and had never really concerned themselves with spiritual practice. They were just a peasant couple, and toward the end of their lives they wanted to do something virtuous before they passed away. They wanted to earn merit, recognizing that, if they were not going to attain enlightenment, at least they could assure themselves of having some kind of positive rebirth. They decided to invite Shariputra to their home. Shariputra was one of the Buddha's main disciples, renowned for his samadhi and psychic powers and for having attained to the state of an Arhat. Shariputra was quite a holy individual and they felt that by serving

him a meal and offering service to him, they would create the conditions of offering positive aspirations and thus they could realize those
aspirations in the future. So with great respect and devotion they offered a meal and some very auspicious prayers and aspirations in his
presence.

As it happened, this old couple had a field of rice which was their
only possession. When the rice ripened the year after Shariputra's visit,
everyone was astounded to note that the actual grains of rice were
made of solid gold. The report of this spread far and wide and the
king heard of this and became quite jealous. He thought, "How is it
that I am the king of the country and have only rice in my fields while
these old people have gold! That will never do." He ordered his men
to confiscate the field and to give a similar plot of land to the old people
as compensation.

The couple were relocated but once they had moved, it was found
that their original field now had nothing but rice in it, and the new field
to which they had moved had grains of gold in the sheaths of rice. The
king moved them again and again. In fact, the cycle was repeated seven
times but the gold would only "grow" where the old couple farmed.
People started asking the Buddha, "What is happening here?"

The Buddha said, "This is simply a case of karma ripening very
quickly. These old people offered their service to a holy individual
with such faith and sincerity that they are experiencing part of the
karmic effects in this lifetime. No matter how much you try and take
it away from them, you can't, because it is theirs to experience." This
was a way for the Buddha to expose people to this idea of causality,
the relationship between our actions and their natural results. These
examples gave people much confidence in the karmic process as a
valid element of experience.

With an appreciation of causality, we can choose virtuous actions
which reinforce positive patterns, producing happiness and fulfillment,
and avoid harmful actions which reinforce the opposite kind of karmic tendency, bringing about suffering and pain. Appreciation of causality also affects our spiritual practice, since it, too, is an action leading to a result. The conviction that cause and effect are real results in
our turning away from negative and harmful actions and toward positive actions and spiritual practice.

There are three sutras which fully describe the concepts of karma,
the *Sutra of the Wise and Foolish* (mDo.sde.mdzangs.blun), the *Sutra on
the Foundations of Mindfulness* (mDo.sde.dren.pa.nyer.bzhag), and the

Sutra on One Hundred Instances of Karma (mDo.sde.las.brgya). These are presently only available in Tibetan, but for those who can read them in the original language, these sutras describe the karmic process in great detail.

The fourth of the common preliminaries is an awareness of the sufferings and limitations of samsara, the cycle of conditioned rebirth. We will examine the concept briefly; fuller discourses may be found in the *Jewel Ornament of Liberation* and *The Writings of Kalu Rinpoche*. Whatever realm of being we are talking about in the cycle of rebirth, it is fraught with some kind of suffering. There is the suffering due to heat and cold in the hell realms; intense hunger, thirst and deprivation in the preta realms; incredible stupidity and predation of one species upon the other—the struggle for existence—in the animal realms; the suffering of birth, aging, sickness and death in the human realm; quarreling and jealousy in the realm of the demi-gods; and suffering of the gods due to falling eventually from that state of relative happiness and ease to a lower and more tormented state of existence. In general when one examines the limitations of the cycle of conditioned rebirth, the cycle of samsara, one can truly see that it is an ocean (or one might better say a swamp) of suffering into which we have sunk.

As human beings we all experience the sufferings of birth, of the aging process, of illness and death. We have no choice; it is part of the human condition. There are many other kinds of suffering which are entailed by being human: the continual search or striving after something which cannot be realized; the continual loss of that which we have attained; the continual contact with people and situations that harm and thwart us; and the continual separation from those we love and hold dear. All of these are part of the human condition.

In general we human beings can be thought of as a mass of emotions. Because there is enormous emotional confusion, there is a tremendous amount of suffering as well. As long as there is emotional conflict, through our remaining unenlightened, there is going to be suffering. Once we have seen that, we begin to realize the hopelessness of trying to escape suffering when we are still caught up in emotional confusion. The only possible escape from suffering is a transcendence of emotional confusion, and a transcendence of suffering is only possible through the attainment of enlightenment.

Let us take the life of Milarepa as a model for spiritual practice, commitment and unflagging devotion. He was able to put up with all circumstances. If he froze, he froze. If he starved, he starved. If things were difficult, they were difficult. He put up with it all and he was able to see through it all and attain enlightenment. That kind of commitment and exertion came from having understood the four basic preliminaries. Because he made them a part of himself, he so thoroughly realized them that he was able to dedicate himself in a complete way. We may not intend to be like Milarepa but nevertheless, in our practice of dharma, we will find that the more we think about and really understand these four preliminary contemplations and make them part of our experience, the easier and more fruitful our practice of dharma will be.

While the teachings of dharma have many blessings and benefits, if we do not have an understanding based upon the contemplation of these four thoughts, then it is like having a finely tuned car with no road on which to drive it. We might be able to get a short distance, but we are not going to be able to drive it effectively, and we certainly cannot get to our destination. Whatever practice we try will be in fits and starts; a really effective practice of dharma is not going to occur without the solid foundation which these four preliminaries give us.

CHAPTER THREE

NGÖNDRO: REFUGE AND PROSTRATIONS

We have explored the ordinary or common preliminaries, the four thoughts which turn the mind away from involvement in samsara and toward the practice of dharma. The special or particular preliminaries of the Ngöndro practice begin with refuge. Taking refuge is linked with the practice of prostrations,* which is the physical element of the physical, verbal and mental aspects involved in taking refuge. The reason we need to take refuge or practice prostrations is because our particular situation is one of helplessness.

Tathagatagarbha, the potential for enlightenment which is the nature of mind itself, is something which is inherent in our being. However, we lack direct experience of it, and therefore a number of levels of confusion and obscuration have set in; we are more or less in the situation of infants, dependent upon our mothers and unable to do anything for ourselves. We have no real control or power over ourselves. Given that we are in this helpless or powerless state, we lack the ability to provide our own refuge, to lead ourselves along the path of enlightenment. The mind itself has lost power to its own projections, to the karmic tendencies that are part of mind, to the thoughts and emotions which continually arise and disturb the mind. Therefore, we are not able to provide ourselves with an adequate source of refuge, or an adequate source of guidance for spiritual development.

---

*Editor's note: This chapter is a complete explanation of the refuge visualization. The reader is encouraged to seek the instruction of a qualified lama for prostrations and refuge recitation (the physical and verbal aspects of taking refuge).

Refuge Tree

In order for us to traverse the path to enlightenment, we need some help; we need to look somewhere outside of our own limited situation for something that can provide that source of refuge. This is the reason, first and foremost, for taking refuge in the Buddha. The attainment of Buddhahood implies the removal of all levels of obscuration and confusion in the mind, and the unfolding of all the incredible potential which is the nature of mind itself. At that point, there is complete control, complete freedom, complete power and capability. Therefore, the Buddha, as one who attained omniscience, provides us with a source of refuge and with the guidance for our own spiritual practice.

Taking refuge in the Dharma, the teachings which were presented by the Buddha to enlighten other beings, provides us with a source of guidance and refuge. Taking refuge in the Sangha, those beings who attain high states of realization such as the ten bodhisattva levels and who realize and transmit the dharma, provides us with an additional source of guidance and refuge. We call these sources of refuge the Three Jewels. Through our own efforts in seeking refuge, and through the blessings which are inherent in the sources of refuge, the connection is made whereby we can make effective progress along the path to enlightenment.

Part of the very compassionate and skillful activity of the Buddha was the tantric teachings called the Vajrayana. These teachings were presented to provide beings with the means to traverse the path to enlightenment effectively and attain that goal very swiftly. A practitioner to whom these teachings are accessible, and who is a fit vessel for these teachings, meditates upon yidams, which are manifestations of enlightenment, manifestations of Buddha in both peaceful and wrathful forms. The *yidams*, or divinities, are associated with certain mantras and visualizations which are used to effect transformation very rapidly. Theoretically, it is entirely possible to attain complete enlightenment in a single lifetime, through the practice of the Vajrayana. Because this accomplishment stems from meditation upon and identification with the yidams, we speak of the yidams as the source or root of accomplishment, and this is the first source of refuge in Vajrayana practice.

The second crucial element of Vajrayana practice is the blessing and inspiration that we receive from our spiritual teacher. The particular function of the guru is to provide us with a link to the living transmission of blessing and experience which has come down in an unbroken lineage. This lineage derives from the Dharmakaya level, the absolute or formless enlightened experience, which is iconographically represented as Vajradhara Buddha. In the case of our Kagyu tradition, one lineage begins with the Dharmakaya level and passes through a human succession of teachers such as Tilopa and Naropa in India. Another lineage begins with the Dharmakaya level and passes through the wisdom dakini Niguma, or through the wisdom dakini Sukhasiddhi. Each of these lineages is a living transmission of teaching and experience from one generation to the next; each lineage is unbroken, composed of gurus down to the present day, and includes our own root guru who is the principal source of blessing for our tantric practice. Therefore, in the Vajrayana, the second source of refuge is the guru.

It is quite truly said in the Vajrayana tradition that the deeper the dharma, the deeper the negativity that we encounter in our practice. In a powerful and intensive practice, there can be very strong obstacles from within and without. In the Vajrayana tradition, there are particular forms which we can supplicate, known as dakinis, dharma protectors, and guardians of the teachings. These are emanations of Buddhas and Bodhisattvas usually in wrathful form. Their principal function is to allow the practitioner to overcome obstacles and hindrances which are encountered in the practice. These forms are described as the root of enlightened activity. In the Vajrayana, we speak of both the Three Jewels and the Three Roots of refuge, the guru (or gurus) as the root of blessing; the yidams or meditational divinities as the root of accomplishment; and the dakinis and dharma protectors as the root of enlightened activity.

Because we are concerned with practice of the Buddhadharma on the sutra and tantra levels, all of these sources of refuge constitute valid objects of our faith and devotion. The benefits of taking refuge are that the practitioner opens himself or herself to the blessings of the sources of refuge. Our minds turn toward the dharma more and more; we become involved with the practice of dharma so that it becomes our path and our way of life. These blessings clear away obstacles to the supreme accomplishment of complete enlightenment. Taking refuge is fundamental to our practice of dharma, both in starting on the path and in following it through to completion.

The four main schools of Buddhism in the Tibetan tradition, Sakyapa, Gelugpa, Kagyupa, and Nyingmapa, all emphasize taking refuge in the Three Jewels and the Three Roots, the six sources of refuge. However, the particular visualizations and liturgies which are used for recitation differ, and it is on this basis that the name "particular" or "special" preliminaries is given to this level of practice.

One fundamental text of the Buddhist tradition states that all phenomena are subject to our intentions and motivations. The way we experience things depends very largely upon the way we intend to experience them, upon how the mind is actually predisposed toward a given situation. In the case of refuge, this truth has given rise to a traditional way of presenting the teachings and of following the practice by which we share the experience of the masters of the Kagyu lineage.

When we take refuge during Ngöndro, we meditate that the particular environment that we are in is not in its ordinary form but is a vast, beautiful meadow. In the center of the meadow there is an enormous lake filled with water of a very special quality; this is no ordinary lake but a magical, miraculous one. The lake is surrounded by a green shore with flowers growing on the banks and beautiful water birds resting on its surface.

In the center of this lake grows an enormous tree with one trunk, which separates into five main branches. The central branch extends vertically and the other four branches extend in each of the cardinal directions. Each of these large branches divide into smaller branches and twigs which are covered with a profusion of leaves, blossoms, and fruit. When we imagine this enormous five-branched tree growing from the center of the lake which is in the center of this vast meadow in front of us, it gives us ease and happiness, and a certain spacious feeling to the mind.

Beyond that, this visualization has been confirmed by the experience of the masters of the Kagyu lineage and we share that experience and receive the blessing of the lineage when we practice in the traditional way. Above the central branch of this tree we visualize a very finely wrought and beautiful throne composed of beautiful jewels and precious metals, which is supported by eight lions and upon which there is a seat in the form of a fully blooming lotus flower.

Above this flower there is the flat disc of the moon, and above that is the flat disc of the sun. In tantric practice these four elements—throne, lotus, sun and moon discs—form the seat upon which we visualize our root guru manifesting in the form of Vajradhara Buddha, the dark blue form of the Buddha. His form is brilliantly clear, radiant and adorned with jewelled ornaments and silken garments. In this manner we meditate on our guru as the Dharmakaya aspect of the Buddha.

Above the crown of the guru's head we visualize the actual form of our guru's guru, and above that guru's form, that guru's guru and so forth, so that there is a progression of the lineage from our own root guru back through the lineage, each figure being above the last. It is as though the figures are stacked like coins, one above the other, so that there is a pillar formed by the figures of the gurus of the lineage. The pillar is crowned at the top with, again, the figure of Vajradhara Buddha, clearly visualized as the source of the lineage. This particular lineage, which is the direct transmission of the Mahamudra teachings in the Kagyupa school, is known as the golden string or the golden rosary of the Kagyu lineage. We also visualize that all the other gurus of the lineage who were not main lineage holders, all of the siddhas, realized yogis, and meditators of the Kagyu school, are grouped around the central axis of the main lineage.

We can then incorporate all the lineages of Buddhadharma, for example, the gurus of the lineage known earlier as the Kadampa school, which was later re-codified into the Gelugpa school; the Lam-dray (Lam.'bras) transmission of the Sakyapa school; lineages such as the Shi-jay Chöd (Shi.byed.gCod) teachings, which were introduced to Tibet by the Indian teacher Padampa Sangye (Pha.dam.pa.Sangs.rgyas) and were developed by the Tibetan woman Machig Labdrön (Ma.gcig.Lab.sgron); the lineage of the Six Doctrines of Naropa, Niguma, and Sukhasiddhi; the lineages of the Kalachakra teachings, particularly the Jorwa Droog ('Byor.ba.drug) or Six Applications, which are similar to the Six Doctrines of Naropa but in the Kalachakra cycles; the Maha-Ati lineage of the Nyingmapa school and so forth.

In short, we meditate on the gurus of all these lineages surrounding the central axis of the Kagyu golden rosary, so that there is a vast assemblage of gurus of all transmissions surrounding the central lineage. The point is to adopt a nonsectarian approach, a totally ecumenical visualization, for while we identify most strongly with the particular lineage that is our personal inclination, in this case the Kagyu lineage, as the central lineage or central axis of the visualization, nevertheless, we are encouraging and developing our faith and respect for all valid transmissions of Buddhadharma without making sectarian judgments.

Of the four main traditions of Buddhism as it developed in Tibet, the Maha-Ati lineages are referred to under the name "Nyingma," which means literally the earlier or older transmission. The other three schools, Sakyapa, Gelugpa, and Kagyupa, are sometimes collectively referred to as the Sarma, or Sarmapa, which means newer or later transmissions. This means that the particular tantric cycles that are emphasized adhere to a later wave of translation of texts from India to Tibet, rather than to the earlier Nyingma translation cycles. The divinities which are associated with the later cycles are particular to these new lineages. In the Kagyu school, particular emphasis is placed upon two cycles, that of Chakrasamvara or Korlo Dompa Dechog 'Khor.lo. sDom.pa.bDe.mchog), and Vajravarahi or Dorje Pagmo (rDo.rje. Phag.mo).

In the visualization, we are encouraged to meditate on one of the forms of the yidams on the branch of the tree closest to us in front of this lineage of gurus. Either Chakrasamvara or Vajravarahi is the central figure surrounded by the forms of other tantric divinities such as Kalachakra, Mahamaya, Guyasamaja, or Hevajra. Any of these tantric divinities are visualized in a vast assembly or mandala of divinities on this eastern branch, taking the direction toward us (forward) as east for the purposes of the visualization.

On this eastern or forward branch in front of the lineage of gurus, the divinities which belong to the Nyingma tantras, from the earlier or older transmission of the Vajrayana in Tibet, are quite appropriate for subjects of visualization as well. In general we find the classification of the Nyingma yidams divided into five groups which correspond to the five Buddha families. Those associated with the wrathful form of Manjushri correspond to the family associated with body; the divinities of the lotus family correspond to that of speech; the divinities particularly known as Yang-dak-tuk are the principal divinities in the family of mind; the teachings of amrita or nectar are associated with the development of positive qualities; and Vajrakilaya or Dorje Purba (rDo.rje.Phur.pa) is connected with enlightened activity. Any of these divinities of the Nyingma school can be included as visualized divinities on this eastern branch closest to us in front of the lineage of gurus.

On the southern branch, which is to the right of the gurus in the lineage (on our left as we face the visualization), we envision the figure of the Buddha Shakyamuni, the particular Buddha who presented the dharma in our period of this kalpa. He is seated on a throne supported by lions and a seat formed of a lotus flower and a moon disc. We visualize the golden form of the Buddha Shakyamuni, and around him are the figures of the thousand Buddhas that will appear in this kalpa. We can envision as vast an assembly of the Buddhas of the three times and ten directions as our imagination can encompass.

On the western branch to the rear, behind the lineage of gurus, we visualize the jewel of the Dharma in the form of books or scriptures. In the Tibetan tradition, these would consist principally of the Kangyur (bKa'.'gyur), the collection of the words of Lord Buddha translated from the Indian language into Tibetan; and the Tangyur (bsTan.'gyur), the commentaries on these root teachings by masters of the Indian Buddhist lineages and the early Tibetan lineages. All of these are seen in the form of an enormous stack of thousands of texts. The Tibetan way of binding a book is to wrap it in cloth and mark it with a small face cloth which identifies the particular scripture. When these books are stacked on the shrine, the face cloth of the book is what we see. We envision this enormous stack of texts, all of them vibrating with the sounds of the consonants of the alphabet in which they are written, so that the texts and scriptures literally hum with the sound of the language which is used to transmit those teachings.

On the northern branch to the left of the lineage, which is to say to our own right as we face the visualization, we visualize the noble Sangha composed of the Bodhisattvas such as the eight great Bodhisattvas, Chenrezig, Manjushri, Vajrapani, and so forth; and the many forms of Arhats.

In the space underneath the branches of the tree, forming a kind of canopy, we envision the figures of the dakinis and dharmapalas or dharma protectors. These protective figures fall into two categories, the masculine and feminine. All of these forms of the divinities that guard and protect the teachings, the dharmapalas and dakinis, are meditated in a vast host or assemblage underneath the tree, supporting, as it were, all of the branches of the tree.

This is a very complex visualization. To be able to visualize clearly all these forms of the divinities with the appropriate colors and the appropriate garments and the appropriate attributes and symbolic implements requires a great deal of stability and skill with this phase of tantric meditation, which is known in Tibetan as *kye rim* (bskyed.rim), the development phase. Even more basically, it implies a certain kind of "Tibetan" experience, a sense of calmness which has been instilled in the mind, so that the mind can hold such a complex visualization for any length of time at all.

Though we might not be able to approach this visualization with any clarity in the beginning, that need not be a cause of discouragement, because Vajrayana is the path which exploits the aspirations that we feel. The most crucial element becomes this aspiration, this motivation that we have. The Buddha himself says that whoever sincerely conceives of being in the Buddha's presence is in the Buddha's presence. We do not need to doubt that. If it is our conviction that we are in the presence of the sources of refuge, then we actually come into contact with their blessing. Even if our visualization is not clear, nevertheless, our basic faith and confidence in the practice and in our ability to place ourselves in the presence of the Three Jewels and the Three Roots should remain unshaken, because this is the crucial element that determines the success of the practice.

Do not think of these forms as solid like stone statues or flat like a scroll painting. They should be envisioned to be perfectly transparent like a rainbow or a hologram, but having no solidity at all. Nevertheless all of the attributes of the divinities, the radiance and brilliance of the peaceful divinities and the flaming magnificence of the wrathful divinities, should be brilliantly clear to the mind, or at least as clear as possible. We then have the immediate presence of the divinities and the gurus and so forth, the sources of refuge, without the concept of them being something real or corporeal.

Dorje Sempa
Painting by Joseph Duane

CHAPTER FOUR
NGÖNDRO: DORJE SEMPA MEDITATION

The second foundational practice is the Dorje Sempa or Vajrasat-tva meditation. The particular purpose of this meditation is to purify us of the different levels of obscuration and confusion in the mind and the negativity and negative karmic patterns that develop as a result of that confusion and obscuration.

To purify ourselves of these kinds of obscurations, confusion, and negativity, there are a number of different forces or powers that have to come into effect. Traditionally these are four in number. The first force is that of support, the basis from which we are working in our purification. The element of commitment on any level, the individual commitment of the Hinayana, the bodhisattva vows of the Mahayana, or the tantric samaya of the Vajrayana, provide this support. This commitment lends a great deal of power to any part of our spiritual development, including purification.

The second force is the technique that we are using as a remedy for a given situation. In this case it is the purificatory technique of the Dorje Sempa meditation, meditating the form of Dorje Sempa above the crown of our heads, reciting the mantra, and using the visualization of the flow of nectar from the form of the divinity to our own form, as a process of visualized purification.

The third force is that of repentance or remorse. This is our sense of regret and appreciation of the negative effects of any given action, tendency, or level of confusion in ourselves, and our sincere desire to remove this.

Finally, there is a sense of promise or commitment to ourselves that, having divorced ourselves from any given tendency, action, or state of confusion, we will not reinforce that in the future. Instead we commit ourselves to a positive direction. This is the force of the antidote. If all four of these powers are present, then it does not matter how deeply ingrained the confusion is, or how negative the particular action is, we can purify ourselves of the hindering and harmful effects.

In the sutra tradition of teachings, we find reference to five kinds of actions which are termed inexpiable. The Tibetan term *tsam-may* (tsham.med) means no interval, because the karmic effects of these acts are so grievous that the consciousness of the being, assuming that there is no effort in purification, will go straight to a hell realm immediately upon death. The mind will experience the negative results of that karma immediately. These inexpiable actions are: the killing of one's father; the killing of one's mother; the killing of one's spiritual teacher or a highly evolved spiritual being; physically harming a Buddha, out of negative intent; and causing a schism or faction in the Sangha, which is the assembly of practitioners. Any one of these five actions is considered, from the point of view of the sutra tradition, the single worst kind of action that a human being could possibly commit in terms of karmic consequences. However, with the skillful use of these four powers of purification, even this kind of very serious karma, which would normally be considered something irrevocable, can be purified.

There are stories in the Buddhist tradition of certain individuals who committed these kinds of crimes and were able to purify themselves of the karmic consequences. A prince in India at the time of the Buddha was guilty of killing his father in order to ascend the throne. He later repented and was able to purify all of the negative karmic consequences. Another individual was guilty of killing his mother and was also able to purify himself through sincere repentance of that act and sincere efforts to purify. Another man whose name was Angulimala was guilty of killing some 999 people. Despite this very heavy karma, he was able through sincere repentance and efforts in purification to purify himself and make quite significant spiritual progress.

In the Vajrayana path, the fundamental *samaya* or commitment that we are observing is considered to be extremely important.* To deliberately violate our root samaya is considered, from the point of view of the tantric teachings, even more serious than to commit one of these

---

*Editor's note: The reader is referred to Chapter Fourteen, "Vajrayana Commitment and the Fourteen Root Downfalls", for a full explanation of samaya.

five inexpiable acts. However, even an infraction of this root samaya in tantric practice can be purified through the use of these four forces. According to this understanding of nonvirtuous and unskillful action, the only virtue of nonvirtue is that it is purifiable.

The Dorje Sempa or Vajrasattva meditation is the single most effective and most excellent practice for purification that can be found either in the sutra or the tantra teachings. A session of meditation begins with us visualizing ourselves in our ordinary form and envisioning that above the crown of our head there is a white lotus flower above which there is the flat disc of the full moon forming a throne or a seat upon which rests the form of Dorje Sempa. This figure is conceived to be our root guru manifesting in this aspect of purity.

The white form has one face and two hands, the right hand holding a golden dorje (rdo.rje) to the heart, and the left hand a silver bell which is held with the hollow part of the bell facing upwards at the left hip. The divine form is seated in a crosslegged posture and adorned with the jeweled ornaments and silken garments of the Sambhogakaya. We envision this manifestation of our guru as completely insubstantial or noncorporeal, like a rainbow, the union of form and emptiness in its pure appearance.

In the heart of the figure of Dorje Sempa we visualize the moon disc forming a kind of seat or basis upon which the seed syllable of Dorje Sempa, a white syllable *HUNG*, is standing upright. Then we envision the white syllables of the hundred-syllable mantra arranged counterclockwise facing outward in either of two ways. If we find it more convenient, we can visualize the entire mantra around the outer rim of the moon disc, surrounding the central syllable; however, this is a very long mantra and, if we find it more convenient, we should envision that it is coiled rather like a spring or a coiled snake with the first syllable directly in front of the *HUNG* in the center of the moon disc and the rest of the mantra coiling slowly outward in a counterclockwise fashion. Either way that we visualize is entirely appropriate.

For someone who has some expertise in the practice of visualization, and faith in the practice, envisioning the figure above the crown of the head is sufficient. For this person, Dorje Sempa is actually present above the crown of the head. However, in the case of beginners such as ourselves, the problem that is posed is that the mind is thinking in terms of this being a mental construct. We think, "This is something I invented, something my mind is just imagining." There is no sense that the meditation is imbued with the divinity.

So, for the beginner, the particular aspect of the divinity that we call forth, visualized above the crown of our heads, is what is termed Samayasattva or *damtsig sempa* (dam.tshig.sems.dpa'). This is the bonded or consecrated aspect, and is our own mental creation, our own visualized concept of the divinity. At this point, we meditate that from the *HUNG* syllable in the heart of the Samayasattva, light shines throughout the universe and invokes the awareness aspect, Jnanasattva or *yeshe sempa* (ye.shes.sems.dpa'). The awareness aspect of the divinity, that is, the actual divinity, is called to imbue the bonded aspect with the awareness aspect. We visualize this by meditating the Buddhas and Bodhisattvas from all directions manifesting in myriad forms of Dorje Sempa; they are absorbed into the aspect meditated above the crown of our heads. We can rest assured that the awareness aspect has blended with the consecrated aspect, and the divinity is actually present above the crown of our heads.

Once we have blended the awareness aspect with the consecrated aspect of the divinity, we pray to this aspect as our guru manifesting in the form of Dorje Sempa. We acknowledge on behalf of ourselves and sentient beings all of the obscurations and confusion that has arisen, all of the negativity that has arisen, and all of the harmful acts which have been committed by ourselves and others in all lifetimes from beginningless time. All of this is clearly acknowledged and sincerely repented, and we offer a prayer to this aspect of the guru to purify us and all beings of this negativity.

As a response to this supplication, we meditate that from the seed syllable and the syllables of the mantra in the heart of the figure of Dorje Sempa, a nectar begins to flow like milk. This brilliant white nectar begins to flow from the central syllables of the mantra and fill the entire form of the divinity. As the divinity fills to overflowing with this liquid, the nectar begins to flow from the divinity's form into our own form through a hole visualized in the crown of our heads. As it fills our form we meditate that this elixir expels all the confusion and obscuration in our mind, in the form of dark and inky substances like soot or dirt. These are expelled from our body through the orifices of excretion, through the pores of the skin, through the palms of the hand and the soles of the feet.

Our physical involvement in this practice is the correct posture of meditation. The body is as erect and still as possible so that the mind can concentrate on visualizing the continual flow of nectar from the divine form through our own form.

The verbal aspect of this practice is the recitation of the hundred-syllable mantra:

OM BEDZRA SA TO SA MA YA MA NU PA LA YA BEDZRA SA TO
TE NO PA TI TA DRI DO ME BA WA SU TO KOY YO ME BA WA SU
PO KOY YO ME BA WA A NU RAK TO ME BA WA SAR WA SID DI
ME PRA YA TSA SAR WA KAR MA SU TSA ME TSI TANG SIII RI YA
KU RU HUNG HA HA HA HA HO BAN GA WEN SAR WA TA TA GA
TA BEDZRA MA ME MUN TSA BED ZRA BA WA MA HA SA MA YA
SA TO AH.

To complete this portion of the Ngöndro practice, this mantra is recited 100,000 times, with additional recitations to make up for any errors. Traditionally, a total of 111,111 mantras is recommended as the complete recitation.

Following this, there is a short mantra, *OM BEDZRA SATO HUNG,* which is an additional mantra used as a recitation for this practice. This is done as many times as we conceivably can, ideally, 600,000 times, with additional repetitions to allow for errors, totalling 666,666 recitations of the short mantra. These would be done in addition to the 111,111 recitations of the long mantra to complete the practice. This, of course, is not done at one time; we divide the practice into regular sessions of meditation during which time we do as many hundreds or thousands of the mantra as we are able.

We will find that if we concern ourselves solely with the recitation of the mantra during a given period of meditation, without any other recitation or talking during the session of meditation, the effect of the mantra will be far more powerful. We can illustrate the importance of confining our verbal activity by thinking of a piece of white silk which has become soiled. If we want to clean it, we need a number of things. We need soap, water, and elbow grease. For the practice to be successful, we could think of the form of Dorje Sempa as the water, the recitation of the mantra as the soap, and the visualization of ourselves being purified by the flow of nectar as the actual work of scrubbing. When all of these elements come together, our purification will be effective and we will experience the benefits of the practice.

In the commentaries on the Dorje Sempa practice, one of the tantras says, "If we can recite the mantra 108 times without the mind wavering, we have become a son or a daughter of the Victorious Ones." This means that the power of the mantra depends upon the mind being focused upon the practice. If the mind is not distracted, then the power of the mantra brings about very high states of realization which will take us to a high level of Bodhisattvahood, and we will truly be a son or a daughter of the Victorious Ones. In the context of this meditation, the only relevant occupation for the mind is the meditation on the form of the divinity, the sound of the mantra being recited, and the visualization of flowing nectar purifying us again and again. Beyond that, the mind should not wander.

At the end of any given session of practice, we offer a supplication to the guru Dorje Sempa, openly acknowledging all the faults and shortcomings of ourselves and all beings, particularly any infraction of our tantric samaya. Finally, we meditate that there is an affirmation from the guru in this aspect of Dorje Sempa, that the form of the divinity actually speaks to us, and says, "O son or daughter of noble family, from this day forth all of your purification has been successful and your obscurations and negativity have been purified." We should meditate and develop an attitude of celebration that this has taken place. This is quite important to insure the success of the practice. All of the various elements and attitudes must be part of the practice because there is an inter-causality between them.

Following this, we meditate that the form of the divinity dissolves into light and is absorbed into ourselves; there is an identity of our own form, speech, and mind, with that of the divinity. We let the mind rest for a short period of time, as long as is comfortable, in the formless state of that awareness.

The texts speak of certain signs that our purification is effective. Dreams of watching the sun or the moon rise in the sky or dreams of finding ourselves in a beautiful garden or spacious meadow, meeting with the form of a Buddha or Bodhisattva, or dreams of climbing a high mountain to its peak, would be regarded as signs that our purification is effective. However, it would seem that the most important indications that we are purifying and developing ourselves and receiving blessings are our deepening compassion for others, our faith in our gurus and the Three Jewels, our understanding and belief in the karmic process, and our renunciation of samsaric involvement. If these qualities are developing, we can take them as signs that our purification is successful and that we are receiving blessing.

CHAPTER FIVE

NGÖNDRO: MANDALA PRACTICE

We can use the example of building a house to consider the attaining of enlightenment. To build a house, we need bricks, wood, cement, and labor. The attainment of enlightenment is no less complex. The Ngöndro meditations were designed to ensure that all the necessary elements in our spiritual practice are present.

Just as we lay the foundation for our home, we establish our spiritual foundation through prostrations and taking refuge. Once the foundation is built, our mind begins to turn toward the dharma, which then becomes our path and our way of life.

The next element is that of purification, introduced by the Dorje Sempa meditation. Now we not only have a basic sense of support, but encourage our own spiritual progress through purifying ourselves of the negativity and obscurations which inhibit spiritual development.

The third element, the mandala practice, is concerned with enhancing the positive, through the development of merit and the deepening of our awareness.

The Guru Yoga practice, which is the fourth element, opens us to the blessing of the guru. All these elements are essential for our spiritual practice to be effective and lead us directly to the attainment of enlightenment.

For the mandala practice as traditionally presented, certain materials are necessary. Two small metal plates which are called mandalas are used as a basis for meditation. The better of these is placed on the

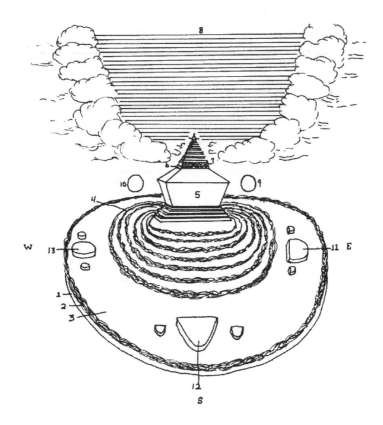

Traditional Depiction of the Main Features of the Ideal Universe, for Visualization

1. Iron Mountain
2. Ocean
3. Golden Ground
4. Seven Lakes
5. Mt. Meru
6. City of Vishnu
7. Indra's Palace
8. Deva Realms

9. Sun
10. Moon
11. Videha and Satellites
12. Jambudvipa and Satellites
13. Godaniya and Satellites

(Not visible is Uttara-Kuru and Satellites)

Mandala drawing by Elizabeth Johnson

shrine, with five piles of rice in a pattern, one in the center and one in each of the four directions. This forms the basis for our visualization of the sources of refuge, the Three Jewels and the Three Roots, in the sky in front of us. This is what is termed *drupay mandala* (sgrub. pa'i.mandal), the mandala of attainment or achievement; the sadhana or actual practice is the basis for that visualization.

The other mandala, which is held in the hand, is termed *chöpay mandala* (mchod.pa'i.mandal), which means the mandala for making offerings. It is on this plate that we place piles of rice in a prescribed fashion and this becomes the basis for our visualization of the mandala of an idealized conception of the universe which is being offered again and again in the presence of the sources of refuge. Ideally we should have these two plates, one of which occupies a position on the shrine and remains there during the entire practice as a basis for the visualization of the sources of refuge, and the other of which is held in the hand and repeatedly cleaned and piled with rice during the practice. If we do not have two plates, we may use just one in the hand. If no plates are available, the practice may be performed entirely through visualization.

The arrangement of figures in the visualization of the sources of refuge is similar to that which has been described in the chapter on refuge and prostrations. However, in the mandala practice, we visualize the lake and the tree in an enormous palace or mansion in the sky in front of us. This mansion is foursided with four main gates; it is a truly magnificent structure, though not something solid or corporeal, but something which is pure in appearance, the union of form and emptiness, like a mirage or a rainbow. This enormous palace contains a vast assemblage of the Three Jewels and the Three Roots, with the central focus being the lineage of gurus surrounded by the gurus of other lineages; the meditation divinities in front; the Buddhas to our left; the text and scriptures of the dharma behind; the Buddhas and Bodhisattvas of the Sangha to our right; and the protective divinities forming an assemblage of support beneath all the sources of refuge.

It is worth noting that at this particular point in our practice, if we have wealth it is meant to be shared and unhesitatingly dedicated in positive ways. Any feelings of being miserly during this practice are quite contrary to the spirit of the mandala, which is why the traditional texts speak of forming the mandala plate of gold, silver, copper, or some precious or semi-precious metal. This is not absolutely essential, and will depend on the wealth of the practitioner. A piece of wood or stone is quite appropriate, but we do procure the best we can for the practice because the more we unstintingly devote our wealth, the more benefit we receive.

To begin a session of mandala meditation, we place in our lap a pile of grain, such as rice, and hold our plate in the left hand. We take a handful of grain and rub the plate, cleansing and polishing it with the smooth part of the wrist, rubbing three times in a clockwise direction and three times in a counterclockwise direction. Some texts present an abridged form of three times clockwise and one time counterclockwise. During the polishing process, we are reciting the hundred-syllable mantra of Dorje Sempa. Our attitude during this recitation and polishing is that all negativity and confusion based upon dualism, in which the outer world is conceived as other and the inner mind conceived as self, is being purified, just as the plate is being polished by our hand.

During the building of the visualization of the mandala, we are placing piles of rice on the plate in a certain configuration which corresponds to the cosmology that is used as the basis for our idealized conception of the universe. We begin by visualizing that the plate is the vast golden base of this world system, this universe. We make the first placement of rice on the plate as a counterclockwise circle of grain around the rim of the plate. We envision a vast mountain range which encircles the golden base; this is like a retaining wall around our world system.

Then we begin to build the actual visualization stage by stage, planting a pile of rice in the center of the plate to represent Mount Sumeru, the central mountain of the world system, and four piles of rice in the four cardinal directions. We take east to be the direction we are facing, so we place the piles in this order: east, south, west, and north. Then in a particular pattern which is learned from someone who has done the practice, we place to the right and left of the eastern continent two small piles of rice representing two sub-continents. We do the same to the near and far side of the southern continent, to the left and right of the western continent, and then to the far and near side of the northern continent. As we place these eight sub-continents, we are conceiving of these as part of the visualization. While we are, from a practical point of view, placing piles of rice on this plate, what we are doing from the point of view of the meditation is creating an idealized conception of the universe as an offering.

Again placing piles of rice in the four directions, we meditate on four further aspects of the visualization to which the texts refer. The first of these is an enormous mountain of jewels and precious substances which is meditated as being in the eastern direction. The next of these is a grove of wish-fulfilling or magical trees that bestow upon the person coming in contact with them all that is wished for; these are in the south. The third aspect is a herd of cows which are conceived of as wish-fulfilling in their ability to bestow upon the person coming in contact with them all that is wished for; these are conceived as being in the west. Finally, there is a field of miraculous crops which grow without any cultivation, giving the bounty of the earth without any effort being necessary; they are in the northern direction. We are calling each of these concepts to mind as we place the grains in the appropriate directions.

The next elements in the visualization are the seven attributes of the universal monarch, the first four of which are the precious wheel, the precious wish-fulfilling gem, the precious consort, and the precious minister. These are visualized as we place piles of grain in the four cardinal directions. The last three of the seven attributes are the precious elephant and precious horse of the monarch, and the precious general. An eighth attribute is a great vase filled with treasure and riches. These attributes are meditated in the inter-cardinal directions, so we pile grain in the southeast, southwest, northwest, and northeast.

Next we visualize eight offering goddesses who offer different sensory pleasures and aspects of sensory experience. The first four of these are meditated in the cardinal directions and the placement of the rice is done correspondingly. The first is the goddess of gaiety and laughter; the second is the goddess of flower garlands; the third is the goddess of song; and the fourth is the goddess of dance. The fifth through eighth of these offering goddesses are meditated in the inter-cardinal directions. The goddess of flowers is in the southeast; the goddess of incense is in the southwest; the goddess of lamps, light, and illumination is in the northwest; and the goddess of perfumed water is in the northeast.

The next elements are the sun and the moon, the sun in the northeast direction, and the moon in the southwest direction, though some texts speak of the sun in the east and the moon in the west. Either one of these traditions is appropriate as there are two valid transmissions of this particular configuration. If the placement that we use is the former one, the sun in the northeast and the moon in the southwest, then in the southeast and the northwest are correspondingly placed piles of rice representing the umbrella, which is a sign of majesty and power, and the victory banner, which is the sign of the victory of the forces of good over those of evil. Finally, as we pile the final handful of rice in the center of the plate, so that the plate now brims over with rice, we are meditating that this fills the universe with all of the wealth of gods and men, and that anything splendid or worthy of offering that could possibly be imagined is filling the universe and being offered to the sources of refuge.

Our attitude should be not simply to benefit ourselves through this kind of practice, but that through this offering and through the merit that it is generating, all beings may come to benefit. In fact, the actual prayers we make when presenting the offering to the sources of refuge state, "Please accept this out of compassion for the benefit of all beings so that all beings may share in the benefits." There is a selfless concern as we are making our offering.

In the sutras, the Buddha described many different ways in which beings perceived and experienced their world systems; all of these are perfectly valid from a relative point of view, from the karmic perspective of the being in that particular realm. The Buddha spoke of world systems which are shaped differently, with spherical, oblong, and rectangular bodies, all of which are possible from the point of view of the karmic perspective of the beings in those realms. The reason why this particular design or cosmology is employed for the mandala is because it represents one of the most balanced, symmetrical, and aesthetically pleasing designs with which to convey the idealized concept of the universe which we are offering.

While the physical object is a plate with piles of rice in a certain pattern, our meditation is that the universe in this cosmology is actually present, and that we are creating an offering filled with all of the splendor and the wealth of a perfect universe. We are limited by our material needs in making offerings to the guru and to the Three Jewels. The most we could ever present would be hundreds or thousands or millions of dollars. However, through this meditative process, we can offer the whole universe. From the point of view of the meditation and the benefits that we receive, if we are sincere and dedicated in this practice, we do actually offer the universe and we do receive benefits as though we had. In terms of the spiritual development that takes place, the difference between actually offering the universe and conceiving of offering the universe is purely technical.

This particular cosmology, then, presents the world system as grouped around the central mountain, Mount Sumeru, which is in turn encircled by seven concentric rings of golden mountains, and in between each of these rings is an ocean filled with vast treasure. Outside the seventh golden ring there is an outer ocean which extends as far as the retaining wall of mountains which encloses the world system. It is in this outer ocean that we conceive of the major continents in the four directions, and the subcontinents, one on either side of the major continents, similar in shape but half the size of the major continents. This particular cosmology is presented as one unit, one world system. The next greater unit of measure for the universe is a chiliocosm, which is one thousand of these world systems taken as a greater unit.

The next greater unit of measure is one thousand chiliocosms. The next greater order of magnitude is the trichiliocosm, which is one billion of these world systems taken as a larger unit. In offering the mandala of the universe we are conceiving of this not as one world system, but a trichiliocosm; we are offering with this single act one billion world systems filled with all of this splendor and wealth and majesty to the Three Jewels and the Three Roots, and the merit is correspondingly great. The farther our imagination can take us in meditation, the greater the benefits that we can receive. Because this practice of mandala offering is primarily concerned with the development of our merit and deepening of our awareness, and because there is an emphasis on offering, then the actual corollaries to the offering of the mandala, such as offering flowers, fruit, incense, and candles on our shrine, are particularly emphasized during this practice.

To begin any session of the mandala offering, we meditate on this extended form of the mandala of the universe, which is termed the mandala of thirty-seven features. We may do it once or any number of times, but the actual recitation and practice that is used for the main body of the meditation is a short prayer of four lines combined with an abbreviated version of the mandala known as the seven-point mandala. This particular offering is repeated 100,000 times, or rather 111,111 times, to fully complete the formal Ngöndro or preliminary practice. The seven-point mandala uses the key features of the thirty-seven as a basis, so that the piles of rice are significantly fewer. One pile is placed in the center to represent Mount Sumeru. Then there is one in each of the four directions to represent the four major continents, and one each in the northeast and the southwest to represent the sun and the moon. However, we should not abbreviate the visualization; we should continue to meditate during these recitations and repetitions of the seven-point mandala, just as we did during the extended form, so that the visualization is as complete as possible.

The particular four-line prayer which is repeated more than 100,000 times to complete the formal practice of the mandala offering, is literally translated as follows. "The golden base is anointed with perfumed water and sprinkled with flowers; this mandala is adorned with the continents and the sun and the moon." The first two lines refer to the structure of the visualization, and the second two lines of the prayer say that by offering this, while conceiving of the realm of the Buddhas (the assemblage of the Three Jewels and Three Roots), may all beings come to enjoy the pure realm of experience.

There are also lines in the liturgy which call to mind the expanded view of the visualization, so that we not only offer this single world system to the assemblage of Buddhas and Bodhisattvas visualized in front of us, but to all Buddhas and Bodhisattvas, all gurus, all manifestations of these energies, all the sources of refuge in all the directions. We are offering millions upon millions of these world systems with this single act of the mandala offering. There is a certain attitude which we should cultivate as a general approach to our experience in the world, particularly when we are practicing the mandala offering. Whenever we are not in a period of formal meditation but encounter something beautiful, a garden or a sunset, for example, we offer it to our guru, to the Three Jewels, to the sources of refuge, so that our experience throughout the day is a constant act of offering.

When we have completed the offerings we intend to do for a particular session, the concluding prayers reaffirm our aspiration that, through this offering of the mandala, we may develop pure merit and deepen our awareness to the utmost, that we may fully realize the intention of all Buddhas and Bodhisattvas, and that we may share in that enlightened state of experience. We affirm that we will not seek to continue wandering in samsara nor seek a selfish nirvana in which there is no benefit for other beings. Instead, through this practice, we will attain complete enlightenment so that we are able to liberate all beings from the ocean of existence, the cycle of rebirth. There are prayers of supplication in the liturgy which specifically call attention to our root guru and the gurus of the lineage as the embodiment of the form, speech, mind, blessings, and qualities of enlightenment. We mentally conceive of various offerings, outer, inner, and secret, which we are presenting to the gurus; and in addition, all of our wealth, body, speech, and mind, is dedicated to the gurus for the purpose of purifying ourselves and receiving the blessing which will allow us to attain the Mahamudra state of perfect enlightenment. There is an abbreviated reference to the Seven Branches prayer of the Mahayana, and we should call each of the branches to mind: the homage we give to the Buddha; the offerings we make; the acknowledgment of our own failings and shortcomings; the rejoicing in the merit of others; the hope that the dharma will continue to be taught; the request to the Buddhas and Bodhisattvas not to pass into nirvana, but to continue to work for the benefit of all beings; and finally the dedication of our merit for the benefit of all beings.

The concluding phase is a general aspiration that, through ourselves and all beings having presented this offering, we may all consummate the development of merit and deepening awareness, and attain enlightenment. At this point, there is an identification of ourselves and all beings with the sources of refuge as the state of enlightenment. We meditate that the field of refuge, this assemblage visualized in the sky before us, dissolves into light and is absorbed into ourselves. We identify our form, speech, and mind, with that of the sources of refuge and we let the mind rest in a state of formless, nonconceptual awareness for as long as is comfortable.

Vajradhara Buddha
Line drawing courtesy of Kagyu Dharma, San Francisco

CHAPTER SIX

NGÖNDRO: GURU YOGA PRACTICE AND GURU-DISCIPLE RELATIONSHIP

The practice of Guru Yoga and a special attitude which views the teacher as guru is something which is particular to the Vajrayana path. In the sutra tradition of the Hinayana and the ordinary Mahayana teachings, when we take the vows of refuge, the vows of a lay person, novice, monk or nun, and the bodhisattva vows, we are not speaking of a guru or lama in the strict sense of the word. We receive these vows from our abbot or preceptor, our teacher or spiritual friend, but not from our guru. On the sutra level of practice there is no sense that the teacher is one to whom we pray as a source of blessing or that the teacher is one from whom we can receive blessing. Certainly the teacher or spiritual friend is considered worthy of our respect and honor, someone to whom we can make offerings and in whom we have faith, but only the Vajrayana views the teacher as a source of blessing.

In the practice of the Vajrayana we develop tantric samaya or commitment with a particular guru through receiving empowerment. This may be a ceremony which involves a form, speech, and mind empowerment of a particular divinity, or a ceremony involving the four stages of the vase empowerment, the secret empowerment, the wisdom-awareness empowerment, and the precious word empowerment. In any case, once we have gone through the tantric process of empowerment with a teacher, then that teacher has become our guru. In a general sense, anyone from whom we have received Vajrayana empowerment and teaching is one of our root gurus. Once that relationship has been established with a particular teacher, then the benefit that the tantric practitioner receives is through the faith and devotion which they have in that teacher. This opens them to receiving the blessing of the teacher and the practice, so that they may attain to high states of realization, which would ideally include the Mahamudra level of experience. This is the function of the guru in the tantric process, to provide the source of blessing and the focus for our devotion.

The particular term for guru in the Tibetan language is *lama* (bla.ma). The first syllable means superior or highest. For example, the canopy which is hung above the throne of the teacher in the Indian and Tibetan traditions is called *la dray* (bla.bres). The second syllable means mother. A guru or lama is as devoted to and concerned about the student as a mother is about her only child. This is the way a guru would view all beings, who are potential students and can benefit from the teachings. There is concern, compassion and loving kindness.

In one of the tantras, the Buddha spoke a certain verse to the effect that the guru is Buddha, the guru is Dharma, and the guru is Sangha. The guru's form is the embodiment of the Sangha, the guru's speech is the embodiment of the Dharma, and the guru's mind is the embodiment of Buddha or enlightenment. So our respect, faith, and devotion are based on the recognition that the guru is the source of the Three Jewels for us.

The guru is the form which unites all the Buddhas and Bodhisattvas and is seen as the Vajra Holder. The term Vajra Holder is a synonym for Vajradhara or Dorje Chang (rDo.rje.'Chang), the Dharmakaya level of ultimate realization. The guru is considered identical with this absolute level of enlightened being.

In another tantra the role of the guru was emphasized when the Buddha said, "Of all the Buddhas who have ever attained enlightenment, not a single one accomplished this without relying upon a guru; and of all the thousand Buddhas that will appear during this kalpa, none of these Buddhas will attain enlightenment without relying on a guru." In order to attain enlightenment, this reliance upon a spiritual teacher, a guru, is an absolutely essential factor.

The Buddha spoke quite extensively about the need for both student and teacher to examine each other before any formal teaching or empowerment is given. The student should intelligently decide. "Is this teacher for me? Is this teacher a good teacher? Does this person have authentic teachings and the ability to benefit me?" The guru determines through examination whether a student will be able to undertake and keep commitments for practice and whether a student is a fit vessel for the transmission that the guru can offer.

Once the formal bond of empowerment and teaching has been established and we have accepted a particular teacher as a guru, then, the Buddha emphasized, it is extremely important for us to have nothing but pure views toward the teacher. Even in the case of discovering qualities in the teacher that we find repulsive, the bond has been established, and purely from the personal point of view of making spiritual progress, the only attitude which is beneficial is to view that teacher as an emanation of Buddha. To view the teacher as an ordinary person and become critical does not help us and in fact can be a serious obstacle.

In general, a guru is someone who is endowed with loving kindness and compassion, and a benevolent, altruistic motivation in teaching. This is someone who has knowledge and experience to transmit, who has understood the nature of the teachings, and has some experience from which they can speak.

From the point of view of tantric practice it is important that the guru also be the holder of the authentic lineage of blessings and teachings that derives from the historical Buddha Shakyamuni or from the lineage which originates with the Dharmakaya level which is termed Vajradhara Buddha. This presumes that the guru has a guru, or had a guru at some point, and that they have had the samaya commitment with that guru. It is very important that our own guru be someone who is respecting and observing their samaya with their own guru, so that this lineage which they are transmitting remains unbroken.

In the Kagyu tradition, we speak of the lineage as a transmission based upon devotion. This lineage originated with Vajradhara at the Dharmakaya level and passed through a human line of teachers, including the Indians Tilopa and Naropa and the Tibetans Marpa the Translator, Milarepa, Gampopa, and the first Karmapa. Throughout the history of this lineage, the crucial element in the transmission of the blessing and spiritual power of the Kagyu line has been the devotion that each lineage holder has had for their guru as the embodiment of enlightenment. The gurus who historically formed part of the lineage of transmission from the Dharmakaya level down to the present day are termed the lineage gurus; the personal teacher from whom we receive empowerment and teaching in Vajrayana practice is our root guru.

During the Guru Yoga practice which is performed as the last of the preliminaries, there are two methods that one may employ for visualization. We may visualize the form of the guru on the crown of our heads, in which case we envision the throne and lotus, and the sun and moon discs, forming the seat upon which our guru is visualized. The guru faces the same direction as ourselves, with the lineage of gurus, one above the other, above the crown of the head of our guru; surrounded by the gurus of the other lineages, the meditational divinities, and the Buddhas and Bodhisattvas arranged similarly to the visualization for taking refuge and the mandala offering. If we find this difficult, we may choose to envision the assemblage in the sky in front of us. They are facing us, so we are in the presence of the sources of refuge rather than meditating them above the crown of our head. Either of these visualizations is appropriate.

The central figure of the visualization is the form of our root guru, with the main transmission figures one above the other, above the crown of the head of our guru, surrounded by the gurus of the other lineages, with the meditational divinities in front of the guru. The Buddhas are to the guru's right, the Dharma behind, the Sangha to the guru's left, and the protective divinities forming a support beneath the entire assemblage.

From a practical point of view, the visualization has not changed from that of taking refuge or the mandala offering; however, from an experiential point of view, there is a significant shift in attitude. When we were performing the practices of taking refuge or the mandala offering, our attitude toward these different sources of refuge was a compartmentalized one in which we conceived the gurus as embodying form, speech, mind, qualities, activities, blessings and characteristics. The meditational divinities performed another function with different qualities. Each source of refuge was considered, in turn, to have its own qualities. In the Guru Yoga practice, the shift of attitude is one of considering all of these secondary sources of refuge as emanations of the central principle of the guru.

Whether we adopt the approach of meditating this assemblage above the crown of our heads or in the sky in front of us, the liturgy begins by describing the assemblage and continues with the Seven Branches prayer of the Mahayana. While we are reciting this prayer, we are ideally linking the contemplation of each branch with its recitation, meditating that our own form is emanated millions of times. All of these emanations of ourselves join together in performing the various branches of the prayer, offering homage and worship, making offerings, confessing shortcomings, rejoicing in the merit of others, and so forth. All these emanations are joined together in making these offerings to the assemblage of the guru and other sources of refuge.

In the liturgy that follows, the supplication to the gurus of the Kagyu lineage is written in quatrain verses, and mentions each of the gurus by name, beginning with the Vajradhara Buddha, the Dharmakaya aspect, and continuing through the line of human gurus down to our own root teacher. We are reminded at the end of each quatrain of the purpose of supplication with the regularly repeated line, "Bestow upon me co-emergent awareness," or, "Grant me the arising of co-emergent awareness." The term *co-emergent awareness* refers to the direct experience of the fundamental nature of mind itself, our own mind as inherently embodying this pure awareness, this Tathagatagarbha or Buddha nature, which we are attempting to discover through tantric practice. So the particular approach of the supplication is to request the gurus of the lineage to grant this blessing to us, that we may come to have this authentic, direct experience of the nature of mind itself.

Following this long supplication to the gurus of the Mahamudra lineage, there is a short prayer which is known in Tibetan as "Dorje Chang Tungma" (thung.ma), which means the short prayer to Vajradhara. It begins with the words, "Vajradhara, Mighty Vajradhara, Tilopa, Naropa," and it is a prayer which brings our attention to the gurus of all the sub-lineages of the Kagyu tradition. We are calling upon the gurus of the four major and eight minor transmissions of the Kagyu school and requesting their blessings for various qualities to develop in us as part of our spiritual practice.

Following this general prayer to the gurus of all the lineages of the Kagyu tradition, there is a recitation of a four-line prayer which is termed the "Four Ma-nam Prayer" because each line begins with the Tibetan syllables "Ma namka dang nyampay semchen tamchay." This supplication is an appreciation of the guru as the embodiment of enlightenment for the practitioner. The first line states, "I and all beings, my parents whose numbers fill space, pray to the guru, the precious Buddha." The next line refers to the guru's mind as the Dharmakaya aspect which is the absolute or formless aspect of the enlightened state of being. The third line refers to the guru's speech as Sambhogakaya, the pure form manifestation; and the fourth line to the guru's physical form as the unimpeded dynamic quality of Nirmanakaya, the physical form manifestation of enlightenment. So in reciting this four-line prayer a number of times, we are calling to mind these different aspects of the guru's being and relating them to the corresponding aspects of complete enlightenment.

At this point in the liturgy, there is the mantra "Karmapa Chenno" (Karma.pa.mKhyen.no) which means, "Karmapa, know me," or "Karmapa knows." The term *karmapa* can be interpreted in two ways. On a less formal level, a karmapa is an activity emanation of all the Buddhas, someone whose spiritual presence is a manifestation of enlightened activity. From that point of view, any spiritual teacher could be considered a karmapa. On a more formal level, there is the lineage of the Gyalwa Karmapas who function as the main transmitters of the Kagyu lineage, from the first Karmapa Dusum Khyenpa (Dus.gsum. mKhyen.pa) to the sixteenth Karmapa Rangjung Rigpe Dorje (Rang.byung.Rig.pa'i.rDo.rje). The Karmapa hierarchs have transmitted the heart of the Kagyu lineage, and this is a recognition of their supreme role. Traditionally this mantra is incorporated as part of the recitation process for the Guru Yoga practice, and we do as many thousands of these mantras as we can, though the formal 100,000 recitations are not necessary to formally complete the Guru Yoga.

Our approach to the guru should take into account the essential emptiness of the guru's mind as the Dharmakaya aspect, the absolute formless level of enlightened experience. The clarity and luminosity which arises as consciousness into the guru's mind is the Nirmanakaya aspect, the form expression of this energy. The Sambhogakaya is the inseparability of form and formless. There is also an emphasis in tantra on the experience of the unity of these three aspects as a total experience of enlightenment, which is inherently blissful. The term *Svabhavikakaya* is used to describe the Dharmakaya, Sambhogakaya, and Nirmanakaya as different aspects of a single experience. In the Vajrayana, it takes on the quality of supreme bliss as the experiential tone of the integrated experience. We view the guru as the embodiment of these Four Kayas, the three ordinary kayas of Dharmakaya, Sambhogakaya, and Nirmanakaya, and a fourth kaya which is this integration as supreme bliss.

In supplicating the guru, then, we are conscious of the guru as the embodiment of all the sources of refuge, the guru's form embodying the Sangha, the guru's speech embodying the Dharma, and the guru's mind embodying the Buddha, the enlightened mind. Also in tantric practice we consider the guru to embody the Three Roots. Obviously, the physical form of the guru is the guru, the source of blessing in the

Vajrayana. The guru's speech is the manifestation of the dakinis and dharmapalas, the protective divinities. The guru's mind is connected with the meditational divinities.

In developing faith in our guru, we are encouraged to consider not only these qualities, but also the kindness and grace of our guru. We consider our guru to be equal to the Buddhas and Bodhisattvas in terms of the qualities and realization that the guru embodies, but even more kind than they are from our point of view. We have not had the good fortune to meet with the Buddhas and Bodhisattvas. Many have appeared in various world systems but we have not had the good fortune to meet directly in this life with one of these and to hear the speech of a fully enlightened Nirmanakaya. We have, however, been able to meet with our personal teacher who, while not being perhaps one of the thousand Buddhas such as the Buddha Shakyamuni, nevertheless is the vehicle by which the teachings are accessible to us; it is through that relationship with the guru that we are personally able to receive teachings, practice them, and attain enlightenment. Because the guru's function is one of leading us along this path to enlightenment, the guru is even more kind and gracious to us than these Buddhas and Bodhisattvas.

There is every possibility that our teacher is in fact an emanation of Buddha, because the Buddha once said that in more degenerate times, Buddhas will appear in the form of personal teachers, and those who come to have conviction and belief in the presence of Buddha in the form of these personal teachers will develop faith accordingly. In the particular times in which we live, it seems that the Buddha was indicating that enlightened beings would manifest as personal gurus upon whom we would rely. Now insofar as our guru may not be totally enlightened, but has an authentic transmission of blessing and teachings from the lineage, it only remains for us to consider that teacher to be totally enlightened, to receive the same benefits as though that teacher actually were. From the teacher's point of view there may be a lack of realization, but if from the student's point of view there is no lack of faith and devotion, then the student will receive the corresponding blessings from the authentic lineage. There is a Tibetan proverb which says, "If we have faith, we can receive blessing even from a dog's tooth."

The prayer that we recite as the main body of the Guru Yoga practice is a seven-line prayer which begins with the words, "I supplicate the precious guru." The second line, "Grant the blessing for the abandonment of ego clinging," is a recognition of our egocentricity as the major stumbling block in our attainment of enlightenment. The fixation on the self as something ultimately real limits the mind to a fictitious concept of the self and prevents our ability to transcend the ego and experience the state of enlightenment.

The third line of the prayer is, "Grant the blessing for the development in my experience of contentment." The text literally says, "No wants, no needs." There is an understanding that it is the basic concept of ego which creates the necessity to feed the ego with what it perceives as its needs, which fuel the samsaric process. With the experience of egolessness, we arrive at a state of contentment in which there is no need to satisfy. The prayer then requests the blessing for cutting off thoughts and attitudes which are contrary to our spiritual development, the mental dissipation and distraction which work against our spiritual development.

Next the prayer asks realization of the nature of mind as being unborn or unoriginated, something which is no thing in and of itself, and therefore not subject to birth and death. The final lines of the supplication say, "Grant the blessing that all illusion, all delusion in the mind, may be pacified in its own ground," and, "Grant the blessing that the entire phenomenal world may be perceived as the Dharmakaya." Through the direct experience of the nature of mind itself, all levels of confusion and obscuration in the mind, which are based upon fundamental ignorance, are eliminated. The entire phenomenal world, rather than being perceived on a superficial level, is perceived as the manifestation of the essential emptiness of mind, and all phenomena and experience are perceived as Dharmakaya.

If our practice is not merely recitation but also a meditation upon these various points and if this recitation is done with a conscious awareness of the context in which we are supplicating the guru, then in the formal practice of 111,111 recitations of this prayer, we need not have any doubt that we will receive our guru's blessing and that the practice will be effective. The point is that the mind must be focused upon what is being said.

At the end of any session of the Guru Yoga practice, we meditate that the figures around the central guru in the visualization dissolve into light and are absorbed into the central figure of our root guru. The form of the guru becomes the union of all of these sources of refuge.

Then we begin a process of meditation which is known as taking empowerments from the guru. We meditate that from the guru's forehead white light shines forth and touches our own forehead. This is the first stage of tantric empowerment, the vase empowerment, which purifies us of physical obscurations and negativity, empowers us to meditate upon the form of divinities, and implants the potential to actualize the Nirmanakaya, the physical body manifestation of enlightenment.

The second stage of the visualization involves meditating red light shining from the throat of the guru and being absorbed into our own throat. This is known as the secret empowerment and is concerned with the purification of speech obscurations and negativity. This empowers us to practice a particular kind of meditation, such as the Six Doctrines of Naropa, which involves the chakras and channels of energy in the body. This secret empowerment is concerned with the realization of Sambhogakaya, the body of enjoyment or pure form level of enlightenment.

The third stage of the visualization involves meditating blue light coming from the guru's heart and being absorbed into our own heart. This is the wisdom awareness empowerment, which purifies our mental obscurations and negativity, transmits the blessings of the mind of enlightenment, and empowers us to attain Dharmakaya, the union of bliss and emptiness.

Finally we meditate that from the three places on the guru's form, these various lights shine forth simultaneously; white light from the forehead, red light from the throat, and blue light from the heart; and these are absorbed into our own three places simultaneously, which effects the simultaneous purification of our physical, verbal, and mental negativity and obscurations. This is the fourth empowerment which is sometimes called the precious word empowerment. It is the introduction to the Mahamudra state of experience, the direct experience of the nature of mind itself. This level is also concerned with the Svabhavikakaya, the integration of the different aspects of enlightenment as aspects of a unique experience rather than separate things in and of themselves.

Following this, we meditate that the guru, wearing a benign and radiant expression, dissolves into light and is absorbed into our own form. There is a complete identity of our own body, speech, and mind with the Vajra body, Vajra speech, and Vajra mind of the guru. We dissolve the meditation into a state of formless awareness and let the mind rest in this uncontrived state as long as is comfortable.

In the liturgy, the recitations that precede the dissolving of the meditation into this formless state make reference to three on-going factors which we attempt to maintain in this meditation and throughout all

of our activities. They are held to be the source of spontaneous liberation according to the teachings. The first is an awareness of all form as
the guru's form, which is to say, the direct experience of form and
emptiness rather than solid form conceived of as something ultimately
real in and of itself. One experiences the emptiness of the form as simultaneously present with the form itself. This is the experience of
divine form, of all form as the form of the guru. Secondly, there is the
experience of all speech as the union of sound and emptiness, like an
echo, not something solid or ultimately real in and of itself. This is the
experience of divine sound or all sound as the speech of the guru.
Finally, there is the experience of all thought and mental activity, all
that arises in our mind, as the union of intelligent awareness and emptiness, the Mahamudra experience which is the experience of all
thought and memory as the mind of the guru. During the Guru Yoga
practice, we are encouraged to develop this awareness of the essence
of the guru in all our activities by adopting some very simple techniques of recitation or meditation which emphasize this.

When we first wake up in the morning, our first thought and recitation is the prayer from the beginning of the Ngöndro text, "Palden
Tsaway Lama Rinpoche." This prayer says, "To the glorious and precious root guru resting on a lotus moon seat above the crown of my
head, I supplicate you to look upon me with your supreme compassion and bestow upon me the form, speech, and mind accomplish-
ments." We meditate our guru above the crown of our head and pray
to the guru in this way. This forms a basis for our attitude during the
whole day so that we continue to be aware of the presence of the guru
in all that we do.

Likewise, before we go to sleep at night, we recite the same prayer,
changing a few words in the second line to indicate that we meditate
the form of the guru in our heart center, glowing and radiant. We go to
sleep with the presence of the guru in our heart. These techniques are
encouraged, particularly for someone performing Guru Yoga practice,
as a way to generate this feeling of the ongoing presence of the guru.

At the end of every session of the Guru Yoga practice we dedicate the
merits and virtue of the practice with any prayers of dedication and aspiration with which we are familiar. One prayer which is very significant
from the point of view of the Guru Yoga practice is the one in which we
aspire that in this and all future lifetimes, we will never be separate from
this pure guru, and that we will partake of the wealth of the teachings,

traversing the paths to enlightenment and attain the state of Vajradhara, the Dharmakaya, the ultimate level of enlightened experience.

The connection between the guru and the student is on a very experiential level. The guru's mind is essentially empty, luminous, unimpeded and dynamic, and this is the ultimate nature of the student's mind as well. There is no difference between the guru and the student from the point of view of the ultimate nature of their minds.

Practically speaking, of course, there is quite a qualitative difference between them, because the student is an unenlightened being, still lost in confusion and suffering, still caught in the cycle of conditioned rebirth and attempting to achieve liberation. The motivation of the guru is a compassionate concern which is continually aware of the plight of the student and continually seeks means by which suffering and confusion can be eliminated. The compassionate response of the guru toward the student is traditionally likened to a hook which is literally termed the hook of the guru's compassion. On the part of the student there is faith and devotion toward the guru, and this faith is the opening in the mind which is termed the ring of faith. With the hook of compassion and the ring of faith, a connection can be made; once the connection is made, the bond cannot be broken until the student attains enlightenment.

When we are pursuing these preliminary practices, beginning with the ordinary foundations and continuing with the special preliminaries, it is very important that we have access to someone who is a qualified teacher. Any lamas authorized by their lineages can give this kind of instruction. People who are interested in doing these practices can receive detailed explanations. It is quite important not to go into this blindly, but to understand the process as we execute the various preliminary practices.

QUESTIONS

In some iconographical drawings of various divinities one sometimes sees a kind of lasso with a hook at one end and a ring at the other. Is that a representation of the hook of the guru's compassion and the ring of the disciple's faith?

The objects which are held in the hands of the divinities are actually symbols for various qualities and one could think of this lasso with the hook and ring as symbolic of the activity of liberating beings, of drawing beings toward enlightenment, from the states of confusion and suffering.

Vajrayogini (Dorje Pagmo)
Line drawing by Cynthia Moku

In the Guru Yoga practice, there is a time when we meditate ourselves in the form of Vajrayogini. Rinpoche, will you discuss this portion of the practice? Also, should one have had the Vajrayogini empowerment to meditate oneself in the form of this feminine divinity?

The texts do recommend that we meditate ourselves in the form of this divinity Vajravarahi, or Vajrayogini, as well as meditating the form of the gurus, the Three Jewels, and Three Roots above the crown of our head. This is because it is maintained by the tradition that if we identify with this divine form as we meditate, we are far more receptive to the blessings that we receive from the Guru Yoga practice.

In terms of the benefits of identifying with a divine form, any meditational divinity would be fine, and in fact we could meditate ourselves in the form of any yidam that we wished. The reason why Vajrayogini is emphasized in the Kagyu lineage of Guru Yoga is because of the central role of this particular divinity in all Kagyu practice.

As a feminine aspect, Vajrayogini is sometimes referred to as the consort of all the Buddhas and sometimes as the mother of all Buddhas in the sense that this divinity embodies the emptiness, the ultimate nature of reality, which generates all enlightened experience. Also, this particular divinity, Vajrayogini, has played a very significant role in Kagyu transmission, and so texts recommend that we visualize ourselves in the form of Vajrayogini, rather than any other divinity, in this meditation.

At this point of our practice, because the focus is on the guru and the Guru Yoga meditation, rather than solely identifying ourselves with the divinity (such as the Chenrezig meditation), we do not need to have received a formal Vajrayogini empowerment. It would not damage the practice at all to have received it, of course; it would be a support. To engage in the Guru Yoga practice, we should have received some form of Vajrayana empowerment.

Can we use Guru Yoga and our devotion to the guru to help us make choices more skillfully?

If our faith is very strong and unwavering in our guru, then there is no doubt that prayer to the guru from that state of devotion can be very beneficial for helping us through any kind of problems or difficulties, including facing a difficult decision. One of the functions of the blessing that we receive through our relationship with the guru is the ability to attain our ends more effectively and to overcome the obstacles that we encounter more effectively. There is no doubt that this can be a very beneficial factor in coming to a difficult decision in our lives. However, it depends entirely upon us having very sincere faith and generating that to the guru with this practice of supplication, which is the Guru Yoga meditation.

When we do the Seven Branches prayer, shouldn't we dissolve the visualization of our multiple selves before we go on?

When we are performing or reciting the Seven Branches prayer which is an introduction to the Guru Yoga liturgy, it is not only we who are giving the homage and respect, the various offerings, the acknowledgment of our own faults and shortcomings, the admiration and rejoicing in the merit and virtue of others, and so forth. We can meditate that we manifest many emanations and that there are millions of replicas of ourselves all joining together in offering collectively this praise, this homage, these offerings, and so forth. This is done simply to enhance the experience of the Seven Branches prayer; we do not need to feel that there is anything so solid in this visualization that at the end of the prayer we need to do anything about all of these emanations. We simply let it go. It is not even a case of returning to being one person; it is simply that it is no longer part of the visualization.

When beginning the Guru Yoga practice, or some other new practice, can we alternate reciting it in Tibetan and English, so we understand what we're doing?

It would seem that alternating recitation in Tibetan and English is quite necessary at this point if people are going to understand what they are doing. You cannot read two things at once, so you are either reading the Tibetan phonetics or you are reading the English. If you try to do both together it is either impossible or very laborious. However, the more we can acquaint ourselves with what we are saying in Tibetan, the better it is. For example, in the lineage prayer, the names of the gurus, such as Dorje Chang, Lodru Rinchen (bLo.gros.Rin.chen), Saraha, and so forth, which are underlined in the English translation, are also present in the Tibetan. We might not understand the particular descriptions of the gurus, but we can certainly pick their names out in the recitation. While we are saying the Tibetan prayers, we should try to be as aware as possible of key words that we do understand, so that it all begins to fit together more. However, to use a system as you suggest, of alternating Tibetan for one session or one day and then

English the next time, would be quite appropriate because then you are getting both the meaning in English and the blessing of the original prayers in Tibetan. The Tibetan is also in meter for recitation.

How can we visualize the gurus in the lineage prayer if we've never seen them depicted?

Even though we are not familiar with each of the gurus in the lineage and the way they are iconographically depicted—the particular gestures, postures, symbolic implements, and garments—nevertheless, what is most important is that as we read through the prayers and the various figures in the lineage are mentioned, we have a sense of the presence of the lineage. We are actually in contact with that living transmission and while we might not have a perfectly clear visualization at this point, we are nevertheless filled with a sense of the presence of the lineage, so that they actually are present above the crown of our head.

At the end of the Seven Branches prayer, there is a request to turn our bodies into the Three Kayas. Please discuss this.

The request to "Grant me the blessing to realize the illusory body as Nirmanakaya, the vital forces as Sambhogakaya, and mind itself as Dharmakaya" is basically talking about the transformation of our ordinary physical, verbal, and mental faculties into their enlightened equivalents. Illusory body means we experience the emptiness of the form, the ultimate nonreality of the physical body, as being based upon the projections of mind rather than as something real and solid. That is what is termed the union of form and emptiness and the particular synonym for that is illusory body. This is Nirmanakaya, the physical form manifestation of enlightenment, and a transformation of our present naive experience of the self.

The Sambhogakaya manifests on our present level of unenlightened being most conspicuously as speech, communication and sound. But there is also the notion of "vital forces." Now the term in Tibetan is *Sok tsöl* (srog.rtsol). *Sok* means life and *tsöl* is a verbal form meaning effort or function; these are two tantric technical terms. The first refers to the prajna in the upper part of the body, which is concerned with respiration, vocalization and speech; the second refers to the lower prajna, which is concerned with digestion, excretion, reproduction and so forth. This is the modal energy in the body. When we think of the concept of energy moving in the body in various subtle patterns, we are concerned with speech and communication as the raw material for the experience of Sambhogakaya. This is what we now experience as ordinary sound and speech, which we take to be something real in and of itself. This is something which can be transmuted into the union of sound and emptiness.

In the final line, there is a transformation of our ordinary experience of mind as something tangible and fixed to an experience of the essential intangibility of the mind which is the formless or absolute level of enlightenment, the Dharmakaya. In all, we are requesting a transformation of our physical, verbal, and mental planes of being from the ordinary aspect to the enlightened equivalent.

Certain wrathful divinities such as Vajrayogini or Palden Lhamo are depicted wearing a necklace of fifty-one fresh heads with blood dripping from the neck. They are variously said to represent negative tendencies or neuroses. Will you please address the significance of this iconographic detail?

This necklace of fresh heads which adorns the forms of some of the wrathful divinities relates to what the Abhidharma literature calls the fifty-one negative mind states. These mind states are directly antithetical to spiritual development. The heads are severed at the neck because the wrathful divinity represents a state of being where these negative mind states have been eliminated forever.

CHAPTER SEVEN
LAY VOWS

All of us are presently experiencing this precious human state of rebirth which we have attained to and which provides us with opportunity and freedom for spiritual practice. It is not something that comes about easily but is won with great difficulty. If we doubt that, all we need to do is to look at the number of beings there are in lower states of existence to realize that human beings are relatively few in number. Generally, human beings appear to all be in the same situation, but from the point of view of spiritual development, most human beings waste their lives. Most spend their lives in idle pursuits, treating the world as something real in and of itself. When we view this reality as ultimately real, we spend our time in a continual struggle to protect and defend that which we hold dear and to guard ourselves against things which threaten us. This kind of human existence, when seen in relation to spiritual development, has absolutely no purpose or heart to it at all.

For example, the average individual feels, "I am a person in this world and this is the ultimate reality." Basing their activities on this assumption, such a person might go into business, hoping to be successful. Putting all their time, energy and commitment into business, they might make millions of dollars and acquire many possessions, becoming quite successful in terms of the world. But ultimately, they have to die, and when they die, they cannot take a single penny of that fortune with them. The mind leaves the physical body. Tibetans say that this is like a hair being drawn out of butter, meaning cleanly, with nothing attached, with nothing following after the mind. The mind goes into the Bardo or after-death state. It is like waking up from a dream; everything that was part of the dream is simply left behind; none of it has been of any ultimate benefit.

Actually, there is one legacy from this life that carries over after death. It is not material possessions but the karmic tendencies that have been established and reinforced through our actions in this life. If these are of a virtuous and positive nature, then the karmic tendencies that these kinds of actions reinforce are ones which will benefit the mind after death; if the karmic tendencies have been reinforced by negative and harmful actions, then the corresponding result will be a negative one or harm the future experience of the mind after death. So the only legacy from this life is a karmic one and the only benefit or harm that we could incur from what takes place during this life is due to the positive or negative karmic tendencies that we have established and reinforced through our actions, virtuous or nonvirtuous, positive or negative, during this life.

Relatively speaking, rebirth in the preta realm is a better state of existence than the hell realms—relatively speaking. The animal realm is a superior state of existence when compared to the preta realm. Among the animals, perhaps the most fortunate and superior forms of animal life are those we see around us, cats and dogs, domesticated animals, and the wild animals in the forests and fields around us. But none of those beings understands how to practice any kind of virtuous activity which would reinforce the kind of positive karma needed to attain to states of further happiness and higher rebirth. On the other hand, the emotional confusion, attachment and aversion, stupidity and jealousy, and pride and avarice which contribute to negative karmic tendencies and bring about lower states of rebirth are inherent in the minds of those kinds of beings.

A human rebirth is a very powerful state where we have the element of free will to choose between a negative action and a positive one. This lends a great deal of power to our activity. But unless we are enjoying that precious state of human existence where we have recognized the human potential and are seeking some means of developing it, we are not in a position to direct our karma.

The Buddha presented a number of different approaches by which beings can develop the means to enlighten themselves. One important element of spiritual practice that he presented was the concept of ordination. Taking precepts concerning our lifestyle can lend power to our practice. There are three levels of ordination, the individual level of the Hinayana, the bodhisattva vow of the Mahayana, and the samaya commitment of the Vajrayana. Among all these ordinations, the most basic is that of the lay person.

In the tradition of lay ordination* which has developed in the Buddhadharma, there are a number of ways in which we can take and keep the lay ordination. Generally it consists of five vows or precepts, of which we may take one, any two, any three, any four, or all five. In some cases, the vow of sexual fidelity can be extended to a vow of celibacy. If we take one precept, we are termed lay people keeping one precept. Taking all five precepts is termed complete ordination. If we extend the vow of sexuality fidelity to one of sexual abstinence, this is termed celibate lay ordination.

The first precept is a vow against the taking of life. When we take formal ordination, there is for each precept a single kind of action which violates the precept completely and terminates the ordination. In the case of taking the precept not to kill, if we consciously take the life of a human being, we have violated the precept completely. This is not to say that taking other forms of life is not harmful; it is in fact a very harmful thing to do, both to ourselves and the other creature. If we take a single act of killing and examine its result, without any mitigating factors, this act can produce rebirth for an infinitely long period of time in the hell realms, and five hundred lifetimes of the karmic retribution of being killed or experiencing short life. So in no case could we say that taking the life of any creature is acceptable, but in the formal context of having taken the ordination not to kill, the only act which specifically destroys the ordination (rather than being a serious infraction of that ordination) is to take the life of a human being consciously.

The second vow is not to steal. This is literally phrased, "Not to take that which is not given." This is quite a difficult vow to keep because it is broken by any action in which we take something which does not belong to us, with the intention of keeping it. This involves any act of theft or stealing, however small.

The third vow is one of sexual fidelity; it is a vow not to be sexually unfaithful to your partner. People who are married, or intentionally live together as a couple, would break the vow if they had sexual relations with anyone else. As was mentioned previously, this vow can be extended to one of sexual abstinence or celibacy, the same as a monk or nun would take.

The fourth vow is a vow not to lie. Any lie, particularly one which is harmful or disruptive to another being, is a negative act. But the specific kind of lie which violates this vow is to lie about our own spiritual attainment, to claim to have reached a certain level of realization when in fact we have not. This is a fairly easy one to keep, I think.

The fifth vow prohibits the use of intoxicants and is considered an auxiliary vow. It is possible for us to take any combination of five precepts; we should only take the vows we feel we can keep.

To take even one of these vows and to keep it well throughout our lifetime is an extremely beneficial and meritorious act. During the time of Lord Buddha, there was an Arhat whose name was Katayana, who was noted for his psychic powers and his ability to visit other realms of experience. At one point he visited the preta realm and came across a fabulous palace where a beautiful woman lived. She looked more like a goddess than a preta. He was invited into the mansion by this goddess-like woman, this preta, and he found the place to be splendidly appointed. He was served very graciously by the woman's many servants, and he spent the whole day discussing the dharma with this being.

Late in the evening, the woman said, "Night is coming soon. I'm afraid I'll have to ask Your Reverence to leave because something quite awful is about to happen and I wouldn't want you to be part of it." He was very puzzled, but he left the mansion and went some distance away. When he turned to look back, the entire mansion was transformed into an iron box filled with flames in which this woman was being roasted, while the beings who had been her servants during the day were transformed into demons of hell that inflicted agonizing injuries on her. She passed the whole night in this kind of torment. The next morning, the iron box reverted to the beautiful palace.

Katayana talked with the preta woman and also used his clairvoyant insight to find out what the cause of this particular existence was. He discovered that in a previous rebirth in the human realm, this woman had lived by butchering animals and selling their flesh. She had come into contact with a spiritual teacher who had discussed the concept of karma and pointed out the cause and effect relationship between positive and negative actions and the experience of happiness and suffering. She became very upset and decided that, although she could not afford to give up her livelihood as a butcher, she could take a vow not to take life during the night, when she would not be working. She felt that she could honestly commit herself to that. The karmic result of this was that she enjoyed the virtue of having taken and kept the precept for the time that she committed herself to it, and at the same time, she suffered the negative effects of the karma that she was accumulating by killing living beings. The conclusion we can draw is that even one vow, taken and kept purely, is of much benefit. To take even one of the lay precepts for the rest of our life and keep it purely is a very positive thing.

Within the remaining two levels of ordination, the bodhisattva vow and the tantric samaya, it is understood that we are taking and keeping these until we attain enlightenment. In the case of the Hinayana vows of individual ordination, the context can be either one of taking them for our lifetime, which is termed permanent ordination, or for a limited period of time, which is termed temporary ordination. The choice of vows and of time period is made by the person taking the precepts and is arranged with the person giving ordination. My personal feeling is that in the case of the lay person ordination, partial ordination of one, two, or three vows does not present a serious difficulty for anyone to keep for the rest of their life. I certainly would encourage anyone who has considered taking any combination of these vows to contemplate taking them for the rest of their life.

There is also a special kind of ordination taken on a daily basis which is called the Eight Precepts of the Mahayana. This is a temporary ordination which is binding for twenty-four hours. It is possible to take and keep these vows for a lifetime, but it involves taking the ordination every morning and then renewing it the next morning. Because these are temporary vows, we can take them whenever we feel inclined. We need only to have received the transmission of the vows once and we can personally take the vows any morning we wish. In Tibet this was quite a widespread custom. Many people would take these Eight Precepts of the Mahayana on a monthly basis or on auspicious days of the lunar calendar such as the eighth, tenth, fifteenth, or thirtieth days of the month.

In the Eight Precepts ordination, the first vow that one takes says, "I will not take life." Because this is a temporary ordination, it should be understood that the stricture of the precept is more binding. In the lay vow ordination, only taking human life actually destroys the ordination and other acts of killing are simply negative infractions of the vow, whereas in the case of this twenty-four hour vow, taking any form of life consciously destroys the precept. The second precept, "I will not take the wealth of others," is the vow not to take anything that is not given to us. The third precept, "I will not engage in any sexual activity," means that any sexual activity with a member of either sex is completely forbidden.

The fourth precept, "I will not tell any untruth," concerns any lie and particularly those about our spiritual attainment. The fifth vow of these Eight Precepts is against the use of intoxicants. Alcohol is specifically mentioned by the texts, but the understanding is that anything which robs us of our reason or clarity of mind is something which is a breeding ground for all problems in regard to our spiritual practice. The sixth precept concerns the use of high seats or thrones which encourage personal pride. A specific exception to this precept is made for someone who has taken the vow but is teaching the Dharma. Out of respect for the teachings, the person who is teaching is elevated on a throne, but it should not be done with an attitude of pride; if there is any pride or arrogance in that person's mind, then this still constitutes a violation of the precept.

The seventh precept concerns fasting after noon. We take a vow to eat solid food up to the midday meal and not to take anything but liquids after that. This is considered particularly beneficial for our practice because fasting and taking only liquids after lunch means that our body is lighter and our mind is clearer. Our sleep that night will be much lighter; the next morning when we awake, our mind will be much clearer. This precept benefits our general health and also our meditation. Finally, there is the precept against personal adornment and activity such as song and dance. We avoid adorning the physical body for the purposes of stimulating sexual desires. The injunction against singing and dancing creates a calmness conducive to meditation by avoiding frivolity, levity, and distractions of the mind.

In order to take the Eight Precepts of the Mahayana, we request them in the presence of a teacher who has a living transmission of this ordination. Once we have received it in the presence of a teacher with that transmission, we are free to take it in the presence of a shrine on any day that we wish. We prostrate before a shrine with representative symbols of the body, speech, and mind of enlightenment, and in the presence of these symbols, take the ordination on ourselves, at which point it is binding for a twenty-four hour period.

The Nyung Nay (sMyung.gnas), which is a two-day fasting ritual of the Thousand-Armed Chenrezig, uses a specific adaptation of the Eight Precepts. This adaptation is utilized because the Nyung Nay is an element in Kriya Tantra, the first of four levels of Vajrayana. Kriya means ritual activity and therefore, in Kriya Tantra, there is emphasis on ritual practices such as keeping silence and fasting. In the Nyung Nay, we keep the Eight Precepts as usual on the first day. On the second day we take the precepts with the additional vow to remain silent, except for the recitation of prayers and mantras, and to fast totally. We take not only no solid food, but not even a drop of water for that twenty-four hour period.

In Tibetan, the word for ordination is *dompa* (sdom.pa), which means to bind or bring together. Ordination is something quite powerful as a basis for our practice. There is the virtue of taking and keeping an ordination and also, if we have some kind of ordination and are observing it, then when we commit negative actions which go against the spirit of the ordination or are by nature negative actions, a confession and purification of those is far more effective than when we do not.

The Buddha said that someone who takes the lay vow or Eight Precept ordination is different from someone who has not taken these ordinations, even though they may seem to be doing the same kind of action. The Buddha said ordination lends one hundred times more power to our actions than if there is an absence of ordination. If someone who has not taken ordination offers a hundred candles or a hundred prostrations, the same merit is accumulated by someone with an ordination offering one candle or one prostration. This is how ordination lends power to every element of our spiritual practice.

The necessity of the benefit of ordination, of this binding or bringing together, as an element in our practice, can be illustrated by the example of a house which has many doors and windows and a great deal of wealth inside. The doors and windows are all open, and there may be many thieves nearby to steal the jewels, money, and precious objects inside. There is a danger. If we could put a wall around that building and close up every door but the main door and keep that one guarded, there would be no danger. Without expending too much effort, we are guarded against losing that which is precious, or being invaded by something which is threatening or harmful. So the function of ordination, of this binding and coming together, is to guard the qualities and merits that we have developed so they will not be dissipated or lost, and to guard us against negative influences that may lead in unskillful directions.

It was earlier mentioned that the fifth vow against intoxicants is an auxiliary one; the four basic vows are the precepts not to take life, not to steal, not to commit adultery or to keep sexual abstinence depending on the choice of the person, and not to lie. The fifth vow not to use intoxicants specifically mentions alcohol, and the reason why intoxicating substances are discouraged is because they rob the mind of its clarity and give rise to emotional confusion in the mind. While in Tibet, we did not have substances such as marijuana and psychedelic drugs, but though the texts speak only of alcohol, it would seem that the effect of drugs is the same, that there is some robbing of the clarity and precision of mind and a lack of the ability of the mind to make judgments in situations. So it would seem that these substances, while they are not specifically mentioned, come under the same general category of intoxicants.

In the Vinaya texts concerned with monastic discipline, there is one known as the *Text for Individual Liberation* which contains stories explaining the foundations of the monastic discipline. In each instance, when the Buddha issued a certain precept, there was a story connected with why the situation had developed to the point where the Buddha felt it necessary to issue some kind of directive to his monks. In the beginning, the Buddha established the four monastic rules: not to take life, not to lie, not to have sexual activity, and not to steal. There was no talk of intoxication until a monk encountered a problem due to intoxication, which forced the Buddha to make a proclamation.

This particular monk was out begging on his rounds one day when he was invited into a woman's home to have the midday meal. After she had served him, she presented him with an interesting proposition. "Now that you are in here, I've got the door locked and I'm not going to let you out until you either have sex with me, or kill the goat that I have in my yard, or drink this bottle of alcohol. You've got to make a choice; it's one of the three. Otherwise, I am not going to let you go."

The monk thought to himself, "Well, I certainly couldn't kill another being willfully and it's specifically stated by the Buddha that a monk does not have sexual activities, so to have sex with the woman would be to break my ordination as well. But there is no talk of alcohol, so it seems that is the safe way out." So he said to her, "Well, out of the three choices, I won't have sex with you and I won't kill the goat, but I'll drink the alcohol." So he drank this alcohol, but unfortunately he became so drunk that he ended up having sex with the woman and killing the animal anyway. It was at that point that the Buddha instructed all of his monks to avoid the use of intoxicants, because there was the danger of it robbing the mind of clarity and giving rise to further problems.

Individuals who contemplate doing the three-year, three-month retreat may choose to take the novice monk's or nun's ordination, or the full ordination of a bikshu or bikshuni (a fully ordained monk or nun), before going into this retreat. This is the idea from the Hinayana point of view. They would enter the retreat as novice monks or nuns, or as fully ordained monks or nuns, and would continue to be ordained afterward because that particular ordination is generally a lifetime or permanent ordination.

Someone who is a lay person going into the three-year, three Month retreat will be required to take a celibate lay ordination on a temporary basis. The five lay vows, with the vow of sexual fidelity extended to one of celibacy, are taken and kept for the period of three years and three months. Following the retreat, the individual may choose to take a further level of ordination, novice ordination or the ordination of a fully ordained monk or nun, and that, of course, would be wonderful. They may choose to keep the celibate lay ordination for the rest of their life following the retreat, and that would be excellent, too. Or the individual may choose to give back the celibate lay ordination and take some alternative lay ordination of one, two, three, four, or five vows. It is entirely a matter of personal choice.

Of course it is worth mentioning that someone who is taking any of these precepts should be intent on keeping them. We should only take those that we feel in good conscience we can commit ourselves to keeping. Within that context, we make our own decision of which particular vows we want to take and can keep.

QUESTIONS

If a person took one or two parts of the lay ordination at one time, could they take additional parts later?

Yes. You can keep enriching the ordination as you go on. You should take just the vows you want to keep and then add to them as you can.

There are many activities we do which we know will result in the death of beings. An example of this would be driving a car, which kills many insects. How is this related to the vow of not killing?

The specific lay vow not to kill, while it implies the conscious taking of any life, is only totally broken by the willful taking of human life. So from a very practical or legalistic point of view, someone who has taken the vow not to kill only breaks that vow completely if they willfully take the life of a human being. Now that does not mean, as we have stated, that other acts of killing are karmically neutral. Much depends on the motivation, because there are different ways of killing. We can take life out of anger, out of desire, or out of stupidity. To take life out of anger is the worst way in which to take life; it is the most serious karmic act. The second most serious kind of killing is that done out of desire, where the motivating factor is not so much wanting to kill that being out of anger but wanting to gain something by that being's death. The least serious kind of killing is the stupid act of killing, where we really do not understand that killing a being is a negative act which causes that being to suffer. If we kill a being out of insensitivity or total apathy to that being's situation, then that is far less serious karmically.

In the case of actions that cause death while they are being committed, where there is no intention on our own part and no awareness of the actual death taking place, it seems as though karmically speaking these are more or less neutral acts. We really cannot expect it to be a powerful negative karmic act, because for an act to be complete, the Buddha described different elements or different aspects of that action. The first element is the motivation to do a particular act, in this case to kill the being, and that is absent. The second element is the object, the being, and that is present. The third is the actual act of killing, motivated by the desire to kill, and that is absent. The completion of the act, which in this case does take place, is that the animal dies. However, all of the branches are not complete, so it is not a karmically complete act. Something that happens as a matter of course, for example killing insects when we drive a car, is by no means good, but it happens. It is not something for which we are personally karmically responsible, because there was no murderous intent and there is no knowledge of the actual death taking place. It is something we are reasonably sure is happening but we do not know for sure. What is most important in our having taken the vow is the conscious motivation: "I will not take life; I will do my very best not to take any kind of life." That is the single most important factor.

If a person has his house broken into, and in defending the family whose lives are threatened kills the person who broke in, what happens to the vow?

While to kill another being even in self-defense is not a karmically neutral act, it is certainly far less serious than to go out looking to kill somebody. If we are not the aggressor, there is far less negative karma involved, but that does not mean that there is none. To consciously take the life of another being, for whatever reason, is a karmically negative act and there are consequences for it. But it is a very different thing to be the aggressor out of malevolence than to be put into a position where it is either kill or be killed.

How could one overcome the consequences of killing in self-defense?

Whether we are speaking of this kind of negative karma or any kind of negative karma due to any kind of negative action at all, it is said in the traditional texts that the one virtue of nonvirtue is that you can purify it. If we are very honest about acknowledging and confessing what we have done, repenting of it and committing ourselves not to do it in the future, then that will constitute a purification of what has gone before. This is the one virtue, if we can call it that, of having committed a negative act; that by confessing and repenting it, we purify ourselves of the consequences.

In the vow of sexual fidelity, do we promise not to have sex with anyone but our partner, or are there other proscriptions having to do with time or place, as described in the Jewel Ornament of Liberation?

While the proscriptions against sexual activity found in the *Jewel Ornament* are intended as guidelines for correct karmic sexual behavior, this specific vow concerns only our fidelity to one partner.

Can we take a partial vow against intoxicants, with a view that we can drink in moderation under certain conditions, or, if that is our wish, is it best not to take the vow at all?

If you wish to make a stipulation which, for example, would allow moderate social drinking, that would be appropriate as long as you have discussed it with your teacher, the person from whom you will receive the vows.

If you do not wish to take a lifetime vow of celibacy, but, because of not having a sexual partner, wish to take the vow day by day, is there a way to do this?

A daily vow does seem to be appropriate in this instance, in which case, the third of the Eight Precepts of the Mahayana would be taken on a daily basis. Ideally this would be done as many days in a row as possible.

What is the difference between novice and full ordination?

The difference between novice and full ordination for either a monk or a nun is basically the number of precepts. In most cases, these are relatively minor or secondary precepts. The basic ordination of the four major vows remains the same for celibate lay person, for novice and for fully ordained monk or nun. In the case of a novice monk or nun, there are thirty, or in some traditions, thirty-three vows which are part of that ordination. These are relatively minor vows when we consider that the basic ordination of four vows, not to kill, not to steal, not to lie, and not to have sexual activity, remain the same. In the case of a fully ordained monk, or bikshu, there are some 253 vows, and in the case of a fully ordained nun, there are some 480 precepts, but, again, these are all smaller or more secondary precepts when compared to the basic four.

Is it possible to receive full ordination as a nun in the United States?

I am not sure if there is anyone who actually passes on this transmission of bikshuni ordination in the United States. This particular transmission of the bikshuni ordination never became part of the Tibetan tradition, because it was never brought as a living tradition from India to Tibet. The novice nun ordination was brought to Tibet, as was the novice monk ordination, and the full ordination of a monk, but the bikshuni ordination did not come to Tibet.

You could not, therefore, receive it from a Tibetan teacher. You could receive it from a Chinese teacher, because the Chinese tradition of Buddhism still has a living transmission of the bikshuni vows, and in fact there are a number of American women who have taken novice nun's ordination, and plan to go to Hong Kong to receive the Chinese transmission of the bikshuni vows, which is a valid transmission of these vows.

The important point is whether we can keep the precepts. If we want them, and know that we can keep them, then the means are available. It may not be readily available on the North American continent, though there may be some Chinese teacher living in North America who can transmit these, but nevertheless there does exist in the world a living transmission of the bikshuni vows.

If your heart is intending to share joy with another person and you are expressing your love for that person, how can anything you would do that would be mutually consenting be considered karmically negative?

This is a complex issue. The karmic recommendation concerning sexual activity attempts to provide some kind of stability, so that our sexual activity does not become the main driving force in our life and a source of emotional stimulation and agitation. Therefore, general codes of sexual behavior which are more or less in accord with the general norm in the human realm are recommended, to try to keep the sexual aspect in proportion with the rest of life. I suppose a certain confidence in the Buddhas and Bodhisattvas as intelligent and omniscient teachers is required to accept that there is some validity to what may seem to be a rather curious or unnecessary stricture. What you say is quite true. If there is basic love and sharing between two people, it would seem that very little that is harmful would ever come of that. It still seems reasonable, however, that we would do well not to be sexual near a stupa, or in a temple, or in the presence of our teachers. This seems to show a reasonable respect.

Many people feel that the prohibition against oral sex is an antiquated cultural attitude that was brought to Tibet and doesn't feel applicable to the American situation. Do we need to abide by this stricture?

There is some basis for this prohibition in the teachings of dharma. However, it seems to me that these are relatively minor points which we could let alone, and just let sentient beings in samsara be sentient beings in samsara. I am not going to be too particular about the whole thing.

I wish to take the vow not to kill, but I kill millions of cells in my work of making medicine. These cells come from pieces of skin and tissue. Are these cells part of a sentient being? I worry that I should not take the vow.

In speaking of microscopic life, the Buddha mentioned the bacteria and microorganisms that are part of any healthy living organism. He described 84,000 creatures living in every human body, and that would seem to indicate that the state of a normal human body at rest is a state of health, without any disease which might increase or decrease any organisms or introduce new organisms. The Buddha did not describe anything beyond these "simbu" or bugs, the microscopic life in the body. As far as the actual tissue of skin, what we seem to be talking about is something that is simply compounded of molecules and atoms and subatomic particles. It does not seem to be something to which we could ascribe sentience.

It seems appropriate for you to take the vow, particularly in view of the fact that the only act of killing which formally breaks the vow is taking human life. If in doing your work you inadvertently take the life of something microscopic, there is a certain amount of negative karma involved in that activity, but it does not break the vow and your initial resolve not to take life would make it sufficient for you to take the vow.

CHAPTER EIGHT

THE BODHISATTVA VOW

The Indian Buddhist master Shantideva remarked in one of his works that this precious human existence, with the opportunity and freedom for spiritual development, is very difficult to come by, and if we have come by this opportunity and do not make use of it, how can we ever expect to come by such an opportunity in the future? The point of this is that the human rebirth that we now experience is not something random that comes about meaninglessly or effortlessly; it is something which arises with great difficulty, something which comes about very rarely. We have the opportunity and freedom to develop ourselves, ideally, to attain Buddhahood, or at the very least, the state of bodhisattva realization. Given that there is this rarity of the precious human state of existence, if we do not appreciate that rarity and that opportunity, and make use of it when it does exist, then when we pass from this life and the mind goes on to future states of existence, how can we expect that that kind of rare opportunity will come about again?

It is said in the teachings of both sutra and tantra that in order to attain to the level of complete enlightenment or to travel the path of the bodhisattvas, there must be an element termed bodhicitta, the enlightening attitude.

In order for this quality of bodhicitta, this enlightening attitude, to develop within the practitioner, a certain understanding is necessary. For one thing, we should have some understanding and appreciation of our own mind in which this experience of bodhicitta takes place.

As well, we should have an understanding of ourselves and all other sentient beings as unenlightened creatures in the cycle of conditioned rebirth. In short, we should have at least some understanding of the state of samsara, unenlightened existence, and of the potential for nirvana, the enlightened state of being. Then true bodhicitta can begin to develop in our mind. Otherwise, it is like shooting an arrow in the dark in the middle of a thick forest. We really have no idea what direction in which to aim and we will have no idea if we have hit the target or not.

The experience of bodhicitta is an entirely personal one. It is our mind which is experiencing the quality of bodhicitta. At the present time we have a vague concept of our mind. We think of *my mind*, but what is actually thinking this? Is it mind itself or is it something different from the mind? We need to understand more about what we are actually experiencing when we think about our own mind.

Because it is the mind which is generating bodhicitta and experiencing it, it is also this mind which postulates its own existence. We need to be able to distinguish between what constitutes the nature of mind itself and the mental constructs that arise from that mind. The Buddha said that we can begin by examining our physical body. For the purpose of this analysis, he divided the physical body into an exterior system of skin, hair, flesh, bones and so forth, and an interior system of the internal organs. When we examine these different parts of the body, none of them individually or collectively is capable of conceiving of an I, of a self, because mere physical substance does not have consciousness. No part of the body, no organ in the body, is capable of coming up with this impression of an I and believing in this impression of an I, because that organ or part of the body lacks consciousness.

The Buddha said that this was true but what is important is for us to validate it through our own experience. When we look throughout the body, do we find that which we can call the self or the I?

If we cannot find it in the physical body, then perhaps we should look at the mental side of our experience. Is this mind which we experience outside the body or inside the body? Is it located in any part of the body? If there is an I, we should surely be able to find it and describe it. If we do not find it, then we might come to the conclusion that mind is empty, that there is no such thing as mind itself.

Ideally, this search is something that would be validated over a long period of time from the personal experience of the meditator constantly checking back with the guru or meditation instructor to get some kind of direction. We would come to a personal understanding of either the existence or nonexistence of some thing that we could call the mind or the self.

The Buddha described the self as purely a mental construct. The mind is conceived of in a way which is experienced as a self or ego. But actually speaking, mind is no thing in and of itself. We cannot find anything ultimately real that we can describe as a self, something tangible, solid, real and internal, something that has shape or form or color or size or location.

The Buddha described the nature of mind itself as empty like space, devoid of any limiting characteristics. Just as space has no form or color, size or shape, neither does mind itself. The Buddha went on to say that the mind is not simply space, empty space, because it would not be effective; it could not think or experience the way it does if it were empty. Empty space, as we know, has no consciousness, no ability to be effective or to experience.

A second characteristic of the mind, according to the Buddha, is its luminous or clear nature. The luminosity of mind has nothing to do with a visual experience; it is the inherent ability of mind to know and experience.

The Buddha also spoke about the dynamic quality of mind, which causes it to be unimpeded or unobstructed in its manifestation. Were the mind impeded in any way, the potential to experience could not translate itself into experience, thought, memory, sensation, perception and so forth. However, there is an unimpeded, untrammeled quality to the way in which the potential of mind can actually express itself as consciousness. The mind can actually perceive form and sound, can make distinctions and precisely experience things for what they are.

In describing the mind in this way, the Buddha was describing something which, in being essentially empty and intangible, has no limitations. Space is all-pervading; so is mind. If we are talking about a mind which is essentially empty, having no shape or form or color or size or location, we cannot then say, "Well, this essentially empty mind of mine ends here; beyond this, it does not exist." Space does not behave according to those properties; neither does mind. Wherever the mind pervades, the luminosity of mind is present. Wherever luminosity is present, the unimpeded or dynamic nature can translate that luminosity into experience. Consciousness is not limited by time and space, ultimately speaking. This is why, even on our present somewhat limited level of experience, we can think of a place like China and an image of that place comes immediately to mind. The mind does not worry about the fact that there is a large distance between here and there.

The nature of mind itself is termed *Tathagatagarbha* in Buddhism. This is the Buddha nature, the potential for enlightenment, which is shared by each and every living thing. As long as an organism has sentience or consciousness, it partakes of this same mind nature. The fundamental nature of mind itself, ultimately speaking, is not something which we can describe in terms of size, or evolutionary level; we are speaking of something so basic that every living thing experiences it inherently.

We describe this pure nature of mind as pure mind, the Tathagatagarbha or Buddha nature. We might think of this for the purpose of a metaphor as clear water, which is inherently pure pristine awareness. What we now experience is an admixture of purity and impurity, of clarity and confusion, of enlightenment and unenlightenment, as though mud had been mixed into the water, temporarily obscuring its clarity.

The most fundamental level of this is simply an unknowing, an ignorance in the mind; the mind is not directly aware of its own true nature, Tathagatagarbha, but instead experiences a level of confusion which is so fundamental that we can only speak of it as co-emergent, simultaneous with mind itself. As long as there has been mind, there has been this ignorance; there always has been this lack of direct awareness of the nature of mind itself. That is the single most fundamental level of confusion in the mind that we might distinguish and it is technically termed *co-emergent ignorance*.

Due to this fundamental unknowing, this basic distortion in the mind, further distortions take place. The essential emptiness of mind is perverted into the solid experience of a self or ego, something central and solid, which takes the place of the direct experience of the essential emptiness of mind itself. Instead, the mind posits a solidified distortion of the self. What would be the direct experience of the illuminating potential of the mind is instead distorted into the experience of something other than the self, something other than the subject. At this point, we are working within a dualistic framework. There is a complete separation of self and other, subject and object. The experience of these two poles is that they are entirely separate and independent of one another. This level of dualistic fixation is the second level of confusion we might distinguish in examining our minds and it is technically termed *bak-chag* (bag.chags) in Tibetan, which means a habit or habitual tendency. The mind is in the habit of experiencing in terms of self and other. Until we actually attain enlightenment, dualistic clinging remains an element in our experience.

Emotional conflict is the third level of confusion or obscuration that we can distinguish in the mind. There is the experience of emotional reaction based on the subject's attitudes toward the object. The most basic of these emotional reactions are three in number. There is the attraction or attachment of the subject to an object that it finds pleasing. There is the aversion or aggression toward an object that it finds threatening. There is also apathy or stupidity in the mind because there is an ignorance of, or lack of attention to, what is really taking place. The ignorant mind is concerned with a superficial relationship between the subject and object, without understanding the essential nature of mind. From the fundamental emotions of attachment, aversion, and apathy comes a complexity of emotional experience. The texts speak traditionally of 84,000 emotional situations which can arise once these three are established as the primary emotions.

Finally, there is the level of conscious activity or karma. Actions which are motivated physically, verbally, or mentally by this emotional confusion can be positive or negative. It is through establishing and reinforcing these positive and negative karmic tendencies that we continue to contribute to the confusion and suffering which constitute the cycle of conditioned rebirth.

In describing this admixture that we experience, there is Buddha nature, the fundamental nature of mind itself which we have termed the Tathagatagarbha. There is also the impure aspect, the level of ignorance, dualistic clinging, emotional confusion, and karmic tendencies reinforced through the actions motivated by that confusion. That is the situation that we experience now, as sentient beings, as unenlightened beings in the cycle of rebirth. We might think of this as mud that has been mixed into the pure water to obscure its original transparency.

We have terms for speaking about these various facets of our experience in the Buddhist teachings. We use the term *alaya* which means origin or fundamental level, and we distinguish between the alaya and the alaya vidyana. The alaya is the fundamental transcending awareness which is the nature of mind itself, the pure mind; the *alaya vijnana* is the fundamental level of discursive consciousness or confusion from which four levels of obscuration arise. Our experience now is a mixture of the pure and the impure *alaya*. The process of spiritual practice eliminates the impure alaya, to allow the pure alaya unhindered expression. The term *Sang-gye* (sangs.rgyas) in Tibetan is the translation of the Sanskrit term *Buddha. Sang* means to eliminate, *gye* means to express. The spiritual process becomes one of removing the hindering factors, so that what is inherently there can express itself without any obstacle.

Of all the emotions which motivate our actions as unenlightened beings, anger and aggression are the most destructive. Not only does anger constitute a main cause for perpetuating the confusion of the cycle of rebirth, but it is also the strongest contributory cause to rebirth in a hell realm. There, the suffering that is experienced is a direct result of the aggression in the mind and the karmic tendency established by aggression. In the Mahayana, the emphasis is upon the development of love and compassion as not only the antidote to that anger but also the means by which the powerful energy that would normally express itself as anger can express itself as love and compassion. We are in a sense transmuting the anger, so instead of becoming the single most destructive force it becomes the single most constructive force in contributing to our attainment of enlightenment.

There are two aspects to what we term bodhicitta, or the enlightening attitude. First is the development of loving kindness and compassion. Second is the shunyata experience, the emptiness of mind and all phenomena. In our present situation, what perpetuates our confusion is our impression that everything we experience is very real. The mind is considered to be something ultimately real in and of itself. We experience the mind as a thing, something solid, and we experience everything that the mind comes into contact with as things in and of themselves. We take the conventional reality to be the ultimate and we remain caught in the cyclical process of samsara, conditioned rebirth. This is what keeps the mind passing from one state of confusion to another.

When we understand the nature of mind and experience the emptiness of mind, then there follows an understanding that the entire phenomenal world is an expression of the mind and nothing ultimately real in and of itself. It has only a conventional validity without any ultimate reality. At that point we cannot help but become enlightened, just as before we could not help but be unenlightened. The attainment of enlightenment is based upon the understanding and experience of the essential emptiness and intangibility of the mind and upon the understanding that any aspect of our experience in the phenomenal world has been a conventional reality without any ultimate reality. This experience of the ultimate nonreality of the mind and its experiences is the ultimate experience. That is what we term the ultimate or absolute aspect of bodhicitta.

In speaking, then, about bodhicitta, we can distinguish the ultimate or absolute aspect, which is the shunyata experience of the emptiness of mind and all phenomena; and the relative or conventional aspect of bodhicitta, which is the loving kindness and compassion that we develop in response to other beings. These go hand in hand and when we are taking the bodhisattva vow we are taking it with respect to both of these aspects. The way that we preserve our bodhisattva vow is through developing these two aspects in our own experience.*

Through understanding and experiencing the nature of mind itself as essentially empty, we come to a further understanding of all phenomenal experience of the mind as essentially empty as well; phenomenal experience arises from the mind and, partaking of its essential emptiness, it cannot be real. The way we come to experience this is to understand that, while the ultimate nature of mind is its essential intangibility, nevertheless there is a misconception that there is some thing called mind and, as a consequence, that sentient beings in the cycle of rebirth suffer confusion.

We begin to see that each being is experiencing what amounts to a dream. When we go to sleep and dream, there is an entire world that we inhabit; when we awaken, we understand that that was just a dream that had no validity on any ultimate level. Dreams are temporary conventional fabrications of the mind, which the mind projects and then experiences as though they were something other than itself. Ultimately, every state of existence that we or any other being in the universe experiences, arises from mind and is experienced by mind as its own projection.

The growth of our personal realization of the emptiness of mind leads us to the conclusion that it is due to a lack of direct experience that we continue to suffer and remain caught in confusion. We understand that, just like ourselves, each and every being is under this mistaken impression that something exists where there is no thing; that some self exists where there is no self; that some truth exists where there is no ultimate truth. Due to those misconceptions, every sentient

---

*Editor's note: To take the Bodhisattva Vow, the reader should seek a qualified lama.

being continues to operate within confusion. This is the fundamental cause of suffering and confusion that beings experience. As we begin to see things from that perspective, we find that love and compassion for other beings is steadily growing.

If we describe mind as something intangible, then it is not something which is born or ever dies. It always has been the case that there is space; it always has been the case that there is mind. It always will be the case that there is mind, just as it always will be the case that there is space. Space and mind are not things that behave according to the usual properties of things which are created at a certain point and exhaust themselves at some future point. There is an eternality to the nature of mind itself.

We might then ask, "Then what is the process of rebirth, which implies birth and death continuously, over and over again?" There is a conventional level of illusory appearance which presents itself to the mind, making it appear that birth and death are taking place. On an ultimate level, however, the nature of mind itself is not something which is subject to a process of birth and death. The physical body that we now experience and through which the mind experiences the world is a result of karmic tendencies in the mind coming to a complete ripening. This is termed the embodiment of complete maturation, but it remains something ultimately unreal in the sense that it is impermanent. The physical body dies, but the mind does not. There is a continuity of mind which carries on from one state of existence to another.

The physical body in the god's realm or human realm results from virtuous karmic tendencies which have been reinforced by positive actions in previous lifetimes. But we can see that things are not quite as simple as that; it is not an entirely one or the other situation, because there may be positive and negative intermingled. A being may take rebirth in the human realm, in a relatively superior state of rebirth, but have a very short life, much physical and mental suffering, meet many obstacles and so forth. These are results of negative karmic tendencies mixed in with the positive. On the other hand, the negative may be predominant and the being may experience a lower state of rebirth in a hell realm or preta realm. Physical embodiment is the complete ripening of karma which brings about a solid physical organism for a set period of time.

Our mind which is now experiencing this particular state of physical rebirth has previously experienced countless other kinds of physical rebirth. We cannot speak even in terms of millions or hundreds of millions; this has been an infinite process of rebirth from one state to another up to the present time. Because there is this infinite scale, we can understand that each and every being in the universe has at some point been in direct connection with us. The Buddha described this by saying that every being in the universe has been our parent, not once but many times. Because there are infinite numbers of beings and because the minds of these beings have been undergoing an infinite cycle of rebirth, the karmic connections that have been established have brought every one of those beings into contact with every other one. The Buddha said that if we were to count the number of times that a single being has come to us as our mother or father, the grains of the earth could not produce a like quantity.

In every one of these states of existence where we have been in intimate contact with every other being, we have received the benefits and kindness that we have received from our own parents in this life. The current situation is that a vast majority of these beings who have been our parents are now experiencing lower states of rebirth in hell realms, preta realms and animal realms; they are experiencing the direct result of their negative karma and suffering greatly. The rest of these beings who have been our parents are in higher states of existence, but are directly contributing to their future suffering by continuing to reinforce negative karmic tendencies through their confused and negative actions. When we are presented with that kind of a picture, we naturally develop a loving and compassionate response to all of those beings.

To summarize, then, the bodhisattva vow is given in the context of these two aspects of bodhicitta: the absolute, the understanding of the emptiness of mind and all phenomena; and the conventional or relative, the love and compassion which is generated toward all other beings. We take the vow in the spirit of developing those two aspects of bodhicitta in our mind, and accomplish this by following the practice of the Six Paramitas or Six Perfections of the Mahayana: generosity, morality and ethics, patience, exertion, meditative stability, and wisdom. The last two, mental or meditative stability and wisdom, reflect the view of the Mahayana. The first two, generosity and morality and ethics, constitute the deportment of the Hinayana. The central two perfections of patience and exertion apply to both categories. The six perfections together will guide us to develop love and compassion and the shunyata experience, the two aspects of the bodhisattva vow.

CHAPTER NINE

VAJRAYANA COMMITMENT
AND THE FOURTEEN ROOT DOWNFALLS

We can examine the idea of commitment and involvement in practice on three levels. There is an outer Hinayana level of practice, concerned with our individual lifestyle as an expression of the search for enlightenment and liberation; there is an inner level of motivation pertaining to the bodhisattva vow and discipline of the Mahayana; and there is the secret or hidden aspect of tantric samaya. The basis for all of these levels of involvement and commitment is the vow of refuge which is the support upon which all these others can be built in the practice of Buddhadharma.

The vow of refuge implies a faith and confidence in Buddha, both as the enlightened state of being and as a person who has attained that state of enlightenment. The more we understand about the concept of Buddhahood, the more equipped we are to develop faith and confidence through appreciating the incredible qualities which arise from this attainment of enlightenment.

The physical form of an enlightened Buddha is marked by thirty-two major and eighty minor marks of physical perfection and these set it apart from an ordinary human's form or even the form of a god in the cycle of rebirth. The speech of such a fully enlightened being is endowed with sixty qualities that make it a vehicle for perfect communication of the teachings. The consciousness that a fully enlightened

Buddha experiences is marked by many qualities which set it off from an ordinary human state of awareness. The more we understand about these physical, verbal, and mental qualities of enlightenment, therefore, the more excellent is our position for developing faith and confidence in Buddhahood as a spiritual goal and developing confidence in the Buddha as a teacher speaking from that state of enlightenment.

Even if we do not have a detailed intellectual understanding of these qualities, it is possible to have the conviction that we are taking refuge in something which represents the ultimate in spiritual development. This is the basis for taking the vow of refuge, even if it is only in the context of this lifetime; we can take refuge from now until we die.

The positive aspect of taking refuge in Buddhahood and the Buddha is the development of our faith and confidence. Taking refuge also brings one prohibition. We are encouraged not to take refuge in worldly gods. No attempt is being made here to decry other religions. The word *god* in this context means a being still within the cycle of rebirth. By definition, worldly gods are samsaric gods. If we take refuge in beings who have not transcended the cycle of rebirth, we have not sought the ultimate.

The second source of refuge, the Dharma, falls into two categories. There is a scriptural or traditional aspect of the Dharma and an experiential aspect. The scriptural aspect refers to the authoritative teachings of the Buddha's tradition, specifically the teachings of the Lord Buddha which were presented from this enlightened perspective solely to benefit beings. The benefits are temporary, allowing beings to find greater peace of mind, or more ultimately, allowing beings the means to free themselves from suffering and confusion and attain enlightenment. All of the 84,000 collections of the Buddhadharma, this vast and profound system of teachings, comes under the classification of scriptural Dharma.

On the other hand, there is the personal, experiential aspect of the Dharma, in which we generate the same experiences within ourselves that are described in the teachings. For example, we can receive teachings for meditating upon compassion, and by using these teachings, can actually generate supreme compassion as part of our experience. We can receive teachings on how to develop our faith and our devotion and, through that, develop a sincere and uncontrived devotion for the Three Jewels and for our gurus. Or we can receive teachings on the shamatha practice and the development of tranquil mind, and experience that stability ourselves. In any of these cases, when we develop the experience to which the teachings refer, then we are taking refuge in this experiential aspect of the Dharma.

Taking refuge in the Dharma has a positive aspect and a proscription. The positive aspect is to recognize the Dharma as an extremely beneficial path and to follow that path as much as we are personally able, through our study and practice. The proscriptive side is that, having taken refuge in the Dharma, we should attempt to eliminate any action in our lives that causes harm or suffering to other beings; we should develop, as much as possible, a nonviolent and gentle approach to other beings in everything that we do.

Finally, there is the jewel of the Sangha, the third spiritual principle in which we take refuge as a practitioner of Buddhadharma. Again, there are two aspects to this concept of the Sangha. There is the noble or exalted Sangha, which is composed of those beings who have attained to the very high states of realization of first to tenth level Bodhisattvahood. These are very advanced if not complete states of enlightenment. There are also the ordinary human individuals who transmit the teachings. They are members of the monastic, ordained clergy whose function it is to realize and transmit these teachings and act as spiritual guides from their own personal experience.

In taking refuge in the Sangha, there is an affirmative and a proscriptive side. We are encouraged to develop positive connections with the Sangha, and to listen to and follow the advice that we receive from our gurus and our spiritual friends. On the other hand, having taken refuge in the Sangha implies that we should not listen to or come under the influence of evil companions, those who would attempt to confuse us or lead us in a direction which was contrary to our spiritual development. This would include, for example, anyone who attempted to undermine our basic confidence in something like karma, saying we can behave any way we like. While it may not be feasible to reject or abandon such a person, we certainly do not have to listen to that kind of advice.

On the level of the Pratimoksha vows, or the individual liberation ordinations, come the classifications of the celibate lay person, the novice monk or nun, and the fully-ordained monk or nun. The term *Pratimoksha* or *individual liberation* which is used to describe these vows also describes the approach. This is a personal lifestyle that we choose due to a recognition that there are certain tendencies in ourselves which are contrary to our own spiritual development and harmful to others. Ordination is an attempt to control the tendencies. There is a dual emphasis, but, because it is from a personal viewpoint, these are called the individual liberation vows. When we examine the levels of Pratimoksha ordination, we find that, in the case of a celibate lay person there are five major vows, four basic ones and the auxiliary vow concerning the use of intoxicants. In the case of a novice monk or nun, these vows are extended to ten basic vows which are expanded in some traditions to a total of thirty. In the case of a fully-ordained monk, there are 253 vows which are to be observed. In each case, the emphasis is on the attempt to eliminate from our lifestyle those actions which are counterproductive to our own liberation or result in harm to others.

For people such as ourselves who are just coming into contact with the teachings and beginning the practice, personal ordination may seem like a very difficult thing. But if we are intent on keeping commitments in the practice of Buddhadharma, we will find on examination that this is the easiest to keep, because all that these vows concern is our physical and verbal actions. There is less concern with motivation and more with how it expresses itself in physical and verbal action, so our attempt to control our actions is completely on the outer level of what we do physically and what we say verbally.

This brings us to the bodhisattva vow of the Mahayana, where the shift in emphasis is to our motivation. The essence of the bodhisattva vow is to attempt to be harmless in all we do and, furthermore, to be as helpful as possible. The heart of this vow is based on our faith and our respect for the Buddhas and Bodhisattvas as spiritual examples considered superior to ourselves, and, on the other hand, our compassion and loving kindness toward all other beings. This vow reaches to the level of mind, not simply to physical and verbal actions.

In keeping the bodhisattva vow, there are two principal pitfalls to be avoided. To begin with, we must avoid developing a negative attitude toward any being, regardless of how insignificant that particular form of life may be. As soon as we have decided, "That being is my enemy and I am committed to harming that being, or not working for the benefit of that being, or not protecting that being from harm if it is within my power," we have committed a serious infraction of our bodhisattva vow. Second, to lose confidence in our ability to fulfill our bodhisattva vow also constitutes an infraction of it. To feel, "This seems to be too difficult. I simply can't work for the benefit of all beings. I better give up and try something easier," is to lose heart in a way that goes against the spirit of the vow. Because subtle motivations are what we are concerned with, it is a much more difficult vow to keep. For that reason, to keep it is extremely beneficial. If we are able to take the bodhisattva vow and keep it in good faith, the benefits that accrue are quite incredible.

In the context of the bodhisattva vow, it is a very serious thing to cheat or deceive those we respect, for example, our spiritual teachers or the Three Jewels. To deceive or manipulate other beings in any way is also a very serious infraction. When we have taken the bodhisattva vow, there is a certain commitment to acknowledge and honor those connections which we have with people, both in a spiritual context such as our spiritual teachers, abbots, preceptors, and advisors; and with people who have an analogous function in a worldly situation, such as our parents and teachers in the world. To enter a situation where we have received kindness through instruction and guidance from these people and then deliberately let them down through refusing to listen to their advice, or by not being honest and receptive to the benefits that we are receiving from them, constitutes something quite serious from the point of view of the bodhisattva vow.

Also, someone who has taken this Mahayana vow upon themselves should attempt to avoid engendering regret in anyone for something which does not require it. Suppose we were to see someone sharing their wealth very selflessly and we were to say to them, "You'd better not do that. If you do you'll be poor in the future and then who's going to take care of you?" To cause that person to regret their generous impulse is something which constitutes a very serious infraction of the bodhisattva vow.

These four injunctions for someone who has taken the bodhisattva vow are known as the four negative dharmas, the four negative actions which go contrary to the spirit of our bodhisattva vow. In the tradition of the bodhisattva vow, we find that the commitments can be quite numerous. There are eighteen further root downfalls of the Mahayana and one tradition adds another forty-six precepts. However, the common point of these precepts is to eliminate from our physical and verbal actions all sources of harm to others and to uproot in our mental attitudes all malevolent or injurious or negative attitudes toward others.

This brings us to the tantric level of commitment, the Vajrayana samaya. We receive tantric samaya when we receive empowerment from our Vajra guru; the empowerment process introduces us formally to the Vajrayana path, so it is considered to be the moment from which our commitment on this level of samaya is effective. Tantric samaya can be a very complicated subject. In the traditional literature we find reference to the fourteen root downfalls of the Vajrayana, to the eight secondary downfalls, and, in some classifications, the twenty-one aspects of body, speech and mind commitment. Some texts speak of such a detailed classification that they enumerate 1,100,000 vows which are part of this tantric samaya.

Atisha, the very famous Indian teacher who came to Tibet to teach the Dharma, is famous far having remarked that when he took his individual liberation vows as a fully-ordained monk, he was able through very scrupulous behavior to keep all of these perfectly purely and did not incur a single infraction of these vows, which was quite a feat. However, when he took the bodhisattva vow, he realized that there were faults cropping up here and there. Because the bodhisattva vow is something which can be repaired and restored if we are very honest with ourselves and acknowledge very quickly our negative attitudes and contrary actions when they arise, he was able, through this kind of scrupulous self-honesty, to recognize these faults when they occurred, acknowledge them, purify himself of them, and restore his bodhisattva vow. Then he said, "When I took tantric samaya, I realized that the number of times when I was actually in letter or in spirit committing an infraction of my tantric samaya was something that couldn't be counted. I was reminded of putting a polished plate out on the ground during a dust storm and watching the dust collect on the surface of that plate. The only thing that kept these infractions from becoming a serious impediment to me was that I was continually acknowledging and confessing my shortcomings and purifying myself of them."

The people listening to Atisha protested, saying that tantric samaya sounded so hard to keep that no one would ever become enlightened. Atisha said, "No, that's not what I mean at all. It's simply that when we are practicing the Vajrayana, we have to be conscious of these infractions and make conscious attempts to purify ourselves." We have access in the Vajrayana to very skillful means such as the Vajrasattva meditation and recitation. A single recitation of that mantra can purify us of a mountain of broken samaya.

On a practical level, the most important considerations for someone who is undergoing Vajrayana practice are the fourteen root downfalls. They are enumerated in a specific order because the first is considered more serious than the second, and the second more serious than the third, and so forth. There is a declining order in the gravity of the infractions from the point of view of our tantric practice. Someone who is engaged in the practice of Vajrayana should be attempting to live up to these fourteen commitments as much as they can in their situation.

The first root downfall is to contradict our guru. Until such time as we have received empowerment and teaching from someone as our vajra guru, it is perfectly appropriate to examine that person and indulge in critical analysis of that person to determine if that teacher is an authentic teacher and a proper one for us. However, once we have established that connection and accepted that person as our Vajrayana teacher, the only attitude that is appropriate is one of complete confidence in that teacher. Whether that teacher is enlightened or not, we should consider that teacher as an enlightened Buddha. If we develop negative views toward our teacher, or abuse our teacher, or commit some action which displeases our teacher, then we have committed the first root downfall of the Vajrayana.

The guru is the most excellent field for the development of one's merit or spiritual qualities, because through one's supplication of one's guru, through faith and devotion, one can accumulate an ocean of merit. The texts say quite specifically that it is far more beneficial to offer to a single hair or pore of the guru's body than to offer to the Buddhas of the three times and the ten directions. One's positive relationship with the guru can be incredibly powerful in terms of the merit and awareness it can generate in the practitioner. In Vajrayana practice, then, once one has established a connection with an authentic guru, it does not matter so much whether that guru is in fact completely enlightened or not, so much as whether the student considers that guru to be completely enlightened. With this confidence, the student can receive the same benefits as though he or she were in the presence of a completely enlightened Buddha.

In Buddhist India, there was a teacher named Shantipa, who was very learned in all of the teachings, but apparently did not have much experience of the teachings. Nevertheless he was accredited as a very fine teacher. One student received teaching from him and went off to meditate on the teaching he had received from this scholar. After three years of meditating on the instructions and teachings he had received, he attained enlightenment. He attained the level of Mahamudra experience, the complete mastery over his mind, and was able to fly in the air due to the miraculous powers he had developed as a result of his enlightenment. Out of very strong affection and gratitude toward his guru, he decided to return to him and to where his teacher was lecturing a number of students.

By this time the teacher had gotten quite old because a number of years had passed, and the teacher looked up very amazed to see this man come flying and landing in front of him like a bird coming down from the sky. The former student began to prostrate to him many times over and then asked for the teacher's blessing. The old teacher looked at him and said, "Who are you?" and the former student said, "Well, I'm your student; don't you remember me?

The teacher didn't, and asked to be reminded of their connection. The enlightened student recounted what he had learned from his teacher and said that these teachings had taken him to enlightenment. The teacher thought to himself, "I've spent my whole life in all this dharma and I have never once sat down to really practice these things and realize them." He turned to his former student and said, "Would you mind teaching me?" He received the same teaching back from his student that he had given in the past with the difference that this time, he actually practiced and attained enlightenment. He became one of the eighty-four Mahasiddhas or tantric saints of Buddhist India.

So, regardless of the particular state of development of the teacher, we should consider the teacher as a fully-enlightened Buddha, because it is only through that kind of positive relationship with the guru that we open ourselves to accumulating merit, deepening our wisdom, developing ourselves, and receiving the blessing that will result in our attainment of enlightenment. To reject our teacher and develop negative attitudes toward our teacher is a cause for rebirth in a state of vajra hell, which is worse than any of the hot hells that are described in the cycle of rebirth.

The seriousness of the infraction depends not only upon the extent to which the practitioner develops a negative attitude toward their vajra guru, but also the length of time that is allowed to pass before we sincerely regret this and try to make amends. If we allow a month to elapse after this falling out with our guru, then this is termed by the tantras to be a contradiction. If we allow a year to pass, then this is an impairment of our samaya. Two years is a transgression and after three years, there has been a definite split.

Up to the point that three years has passed from the time we first developed these attitudes, it is quite possible for us to repair the damage. We can confess and acknowledge this fault that has occurred and we can purify ourselves and attempt to re-establish a positive bond with our teacher. However, if we have allowed more than three years to elapse, from the point of view of the tantra, the situation is probably hopeless. We have allowed far too long a time to elapse and the bond is irreparable. The texts speak of no direction for such a consciousness but vajra hell.

The texts also speak of specific means that we should adopt to repair this bond, depending on the severity and the length of time. If we have committed a contradiction through allowing a month to pass, then we should offer to our teacher a ganachakra, a vajra feast to purify ourselves of this transgression of our samaya. If we have allowed an impairment to remain for one year, then we should offer all of our possessions to our guru. If we have allowed two years to expire, so that a transgression has occurred, then we should offer our family, our children, our spouse and whatever we have, to the guru to purify ourselves and to restore this positive connection. If we have allowed three years to expire following this first root downfall of the Vajrayana, we should be prepared to offer our life to restore the bond with the guru.

The second root downfall of the Vajrayana is to contradict or refute the teachings of Buddha or the personal teachings that we receive from our guru. What this implies is that we should do what our guru tells us to do, or at least the best we can. For this reason, when I am teaching as a guru, I am careful to present things in such a way that I encourage people to practice as much virtue as they are able, and to avoid as much negative and harmful activity as they are able to, and I tend to avoid laying down strict injunctions that we must do this or we must not do that, because I do not want to put people in the position where they may be incurring this kind of fault through me having put them in an impossible situation. I encourage people to do the best they can. For example, I encourage all of you who are my students to use the Chenrezig meditation and to recite the mantra OM MANI PADME HUNG as much as possible, because I feel that this is perhaps the single most beneficial technique and instruction that I can give to you. I am not trying to start a fan club, so that the more people who practice Chenrezig, the more famous I become or the more people hold me up as some kind of shining example. It is simply because I feel this is the most beneficial.

The third root downfall of the Vajrayana concerns our relationship with our vajra brothers and sisters, all those men and women with whom we are connected through having received empowerments from the same teachers or in the same mandala. The only relationship that is appropriate within the context of samaya is a harmonious and mutually helpful relationship between ourselves and our vajra brothers and sisters. Quarreling, spite, competitiveness, malevolent attitudes toward each other, bickering, and discord between ourselves and these people are completely out of the question from the point of view of samaya. We must respect the very important bond that we have with these people through our commitment to Vajrayana. The bond exists and we must attempt to promote harmony and mutual accord, mutual help and benefit, as much as possible among the vajra sangha.

In general, of course, all sentient beings are our brothers and sisters; we are connected to each and every living thing. However, on a more formal level, all those who are involved in the practice of Buddhadharma are more intimately connected with ourselves, and particularly those who are involved in Vajrayana practice. Those people who share the same guru share the same spiritual father. Those who have received empowerment in the same mandala, though perhaps with different teachers, share the same spiritual mother, from the point of view of tantra. Those who have received the same empowerment from the same teacher have the single most intimate bond possible. They are Vajrayana brothers and sisters with the same spiritual father and mother.

The fourth root downfall is the breaking of our bodhisattva vow. To develop an injurious or negative attitude toward any being, no matter how insignificant; to harm, to avoid protecting, or to avoid benefitting any being if we can, not only violates our bodhisattva vow on a very fundamental level, but from the point of view of tantric practice violates the fourth root downfall.

In the practice of Vajrayana, these first four precepts are the most crucial from the point of view of the importance of keeping them and the seriousness of contradicting them. Whether we contradict our guru, which is the most serious downfall from the point of view of tantric practices; whether we are contradicting the teachings that we have received; or contradicting our vajra brothers and sisters or other beings, or breaking the bodhisattva vow, we are seriously violating our tantric samaya.

The fifth root downfall in the Vajrayana concerns the impairment of two forces in our bodies which are termed the white and red bindu; these are intimately connected with the sexual processes of our bodies. In Mahamudra meditation, particularly when we are using the *tsa-lung* (rtsa.rlung) techniques which deal with chakras and the prajna which moves in various channels, these white and red bindu are the basis of the development for bliss and emptiness in meditation. Because there is an emphasis on the preservation of these bindu for proper practice, there is a recommendation that the tantric practitioner avoid damaging or impairing these forces through sexual activity.

The sixth root downfall concerns our own and others' spiritual systems. From the point of view of Vajrayana, it is a root downfall to denigrate or abuse any spiritual system, regardless of whether it is Buddhist or non-Buddhist. Of course, in the context of the Tibetan tradition, we may find criticism between the various schools, Sakyapa, Gelugpa, Kagyupa, and Nyingmapa, and that is foolish and harmful from the point of view of our spiritual practice. But in the case of Vajrayana practice, this prohibition extends to other religions as well, so that a tantric practitioner is not only to avoid disparaging any tradition of Buddhadharma but also Hinduism, Judaism, Christianity, Islam, and other spiritual systems.

The seventh vow concerns the revealing of secret teachings to those who are not fit to receive them, which means discussing very profound and secret concepts of Vajrayana practice with those who are not prepared to accept them, who openly reject them, or who are not prepared to involve themselves with the tantric process in any way.

The eighth root downfall is to regard our physical bodies, or the skandhas or aggregates of our psycho-physical makeup, as impure and base. The reason why this is a root downfall is because Vajrayana sees everything as sacred. All appearance is a form of divinity, all sound is the sound of mantra, and all thought and awareness is the divine play of transcending awareness, the Mahamudra experience. The potential for that sacredness exists within our present framework, so to speak, of the five skandhas. Acknowledging psycho-physical aggregates of an individual as the potential of the Buddhas of the five families, or the five elements, or the five feminine aspects, and so forth, is to recognize that, in tantra, the potential for that transformation exists within our present situation. To disparage that potential as something useless or impure or unwholesome is a root downfall, a basic contradiction, from the point of view of tantric practice.

The ninth root downfall from the point of view of Vajrayana is to entertain doubts or hesitations about our own involvement in tantric practice. We should have complete confidence, ideally, in what we are doing in tantra and not think, "Well, perhaps this is beneficial, but then again, I'm not sure. Maybe to meditate upon this divinity is going to be helpful but maybe it's a waste of time." This ambivalent attitude toward our practice is a basic contradiction to the path.

The tenth root downfall is something which would not seem to apply very much in our case, but it is worth mentioning. The texts say that in certain situations, if there are beings who are behaving in extremely evil ways and committing extremely negative karma, which inevitably will send them to a lower state of rebirth and cause infinite harm to other beings, it is possible for an advanced tantric practitioner, in a state of supreme compassion, to terminate that being's existence and liberate them from their state of very negative existence. It must be done totally selflessly, from absolute compassion, understanding, and control of the situation; hence, it would not seem to apply in our case. However, from the point of view of tantric practice, if one has the ability to take this action and refuses to bring a halt to terrible harm when one could alter it in a very beneficial way, then one is committing the tenth root downfall.

The eleventh root downfall of the Vajrayana concerns extremes in our outlook or view. There are two extremes to avoid. We can either be a naive realist and assume that everything that we experience is absolutely real with no possibility of any other ultimate reality; or we can take the description of shunyata to be a negation of everything, and believe that nothing exists, nothing is true and karma is completely false. To fall into either of these extremes, naive realism or naive nihilism, is not following the correct view for tantric practice, and therefore constitutes the eleventh root downfall.

The twelfth root downfall is to refuse to teach a sincere and interested individual who comes to us in the context of receiving teaching with faith. If we are able to teach that person and if we renege and do not teach, we are committing this twelfth root downfall.

The thirteenth root downfall concerns our attitude and approach to tantric practice and tantric ritual. If we are participating in a ganachakra or vajra feast, where the ritual use of meat and alcohol is made, and we abstain from one or the other of these on the grounds that it is impure or that it is contrary to our convictions and principles, then we have failed to appreciate the view of tantra which attempts to transcend purity and impurity, attempts to transcend dualistic thinking, and we have failed to appreciate and take part in the spirit of that tantric transformation process. To indulge in this kind of superficial, dualistic clinging to appearances during the course of a tantric ritual is to commit this thirteenth root downfall and to go against the spirit of our tantric practice.

The fourteenth root downfall is to disparage women, either by a mental attitude of considering women to be lower than men or by verbalizing these opinions.

These are the fourteen root downfalls of Vajrayana practice; there are many auxiliary or secondary aspects to these which will not be described here. From the positive view, in tantric practice the attempt is to absorb ourselves physically, verbally and mentally in an ongoing way, so that our perception of form is never separate from the awareness of the form of the divinity; our perception of sound and speech is not separate from our perception of the mantra; and our mental experience of thoughts, memories, concepts, and emotions is not separate from the state of samadhi. If we are able to absorb ourselves in an ongoing way on these levels of form, speech and mind, then all of these 1,100,000 vows of samaya are kept perfectly.

There is a famous story in Tibet of a teacher who is talking about negative and positive action, virtuous and nonvirtuous karma. An old woman who was in the audience got up and said, "You know, Rinpoche, when you speak about the benefits of practicing virtue, I feel that not only are you enlightened, but I am, too. Me, this old woman. But then you talk about all the negative aspects of harmful and nonvirtuous action, and I feel that not only am I doomed, but you are really in trouble, too."

This is a brief discussion of the Hinayana, Mahayana and Vajrayana levels of commitment, that is, the individual liberation vows, the bodhisattva vow, and tantric samaya. As I mentioned earlier, if we are sincerely trying physically, verbally and mentally to develop as much virtue in ourselves, and to eliminate as much negativity, then, from the point of view of the practice of Buddhadharma, we are doing our best and that is sufficient.

CHAPTER TEN

SHAMATHA PRACTICE: OBJECT MEDITATION

There are many techniques that we can use to develop tranquility and stability of mind. For example, we can meditate on the form of a divinity, or we can focus the mind on the form of a seed syllable or a physical object such as a piece of wood or a stone. Theoretically speaking, there is no reason why any physical object could not be used as a basis or support for meditation. We could rest the mind upon the experience of seeing a particular form and any of these objects could be effective for developing shamatha, the tranquility and stability of mind. A very effective technique which we will explore in this chapter is to meditate upon bindu, which means to meditate upon a small sphere of light.

Meditation is a mental practice, whether we use the basic shamatha approach to instill tranquility and stability to the mind; or a vipasyana approach to develop insight into the nature of the mind; or a Mahayana technique to develop compassion and shunyata; or tantric phases of creation and fulfillment. It is with the mind that we meditate so we must begin with the nature of the mind itself. The more we understand, the more beneficial a particular technique will be.

When we speak of mind, we are not speaking about an object. Ultimately speaking, we cannot describe the mind, or consciousness, in terms of being some thing. The nature of mind itself is nothingness, emptiness; and the mind exhibits no fixed or limiting characteristics such as form, color, shape, size or location. Mind exhibits an intangibility which we compare to space as having no parameters or boundaries.

In allowing oneself to experience the spacious and intangible quality of the nature of mind, physical posture is an important factor. The body should be held erect, without being rigid or tense. The mind should rest in its natural state. There is no need to consider the mind as being outside or inside the body. There is no need to focus the attention toward one direction or another. All that is necessary is to let the mind rest in the spacious experience of mind itself, without any distraction, contrivance or artifice.

Since the mind cannot be experienced as tangible or limited, we should not say, "My mind extends only so far and beyond that, it is no longer present or valid." There is no arbitrary boundary beyond which the mind is absent and within which the mind is present. It does not behave according to those parameters. However, because we lack direct experience of the fundamental intangibility of mind, we tend to perceive the mind as though it were limited and fixed. We have a naive conception of I, my mind, my body, and think that the mind is located in the body somewhere. We behave according to the misconception that the mind is something that we can fix or limit or pin down.

The mind is also luminous, not in the visual sense but in that it can perceive anything. This luminosity is simultaneously present with intangible emptiness; they are not two separate things but two aspects of the same experience.

This experience of simultaneous emptiness and luminosity has the ability to manifest dynamically and unimpededly, as intelligent awareness. This cognitive aspect of mind not only can, but does, perceive and experience. In our particular case, the cognitive aspect of mind takes the form of five physical senses and the inner consciousness which produces thoughts and ideas as a kind of sixth sense. If we take the physical sense of hearing, for example, we have the empty and luminous nature of mind expressing itself through the avenue we term auditory consciousness. The ear is merely the particular physical organ which acts as a vehicle by which consciousness can express itself. There are different elements present when we perceive sound. Consciousness expresses itself as auditory awareness and the physical organ acts as the link between the subjective consciousness and what is perceived as the objective element, the sound in the physical environment. What is actually taking place is a manifestation of the empty, luminous and unimpeded nature of mind itself.

If we practice shamatha meditation by using some reference point in the phenomenal environment, then we incorporate the object, the organ or avenue of consciousness, and consciousness itself. These three factors come together as the perceptual situation. Using this perceptual situation of sensory object, sensory organ or avenue, and consciousness or cognition, this particular situation can give rise to a number of different levels of realization and experience. It may instill a calm stability to mind. In this case it is shamatha meditation. It may instill a certain insight and partial realization, though not what we would call complete enlightenment. This is vipasyana meditation. When one has attained complete enlightenment, and a perceptual situation is simply an expression of that enlightened being, then we are speaking of Mahamudra. So a perceptual situation can be, from the point of view of the practitioner, a shamatha or tranquility experience; an experience of insight or vipasyana; or the Mahamudra experience, the direct and ultimate experience of the nature of mind and all phenomena.

When we use the technique of shamatha with an object, a focal point, then we are using a kind of perceptual situation. If we meditate on a statue of the Buddha, for example, then there is an object in the environment, there is the vehicle or avenue for the consciousness (in this case the eyes or organs of sight), and there is the consciousness itself, the cognitive factor of mind's awareness presenting itself through the organ of sight as the visual experience of that particular object.

If we use a purely mental approach, in which there is no physical object in the environment, but create a mental object such as a ball of light or the form of a divinity, the situation is the same. There is the object, in this case not perceived as physically present in the external environment but nevertheless something upon which the mind focuses as an object. There is the sixth sense of inner consciousness, not a physical sense of sight or sound but the mind functioning as a sensory organ to produce objects. Finally, there is consciousness itself, the empty, luminous and unimpeded state of awareness expressing itself through inner consciousness to perceive the mental object. Meditation on the form of the divinity or a small ball of light utilizes the same approach.

In the literature of the Prajnaparamita, the Perfection of Wisdom, there is a passage which states, "First there is I and everything else develops from the sense of I." From this basic assumption of *I* or self develops my body, my mind, my this, my that; and the whole world develops from that belief.

Because there is this habitual tendency of the mind to experience in terms of I and mine, fixating on the mind as being located in the body, we can use this as a vehicle for meditation. We can conceive of an object for meditation in the form of a globe or sphere of light which is visualized as being present within the body, perhaps in the heart region. We focus the mind, which is always concentrating on the self and the body anyway, and bring it to bear on this sphere of light which we place in the heart region of the body. Both the sphere of light and that which is aware of the sphere are the expression of the empty, clear and unimpeded nature of mind. This is something which is quite important to understand. The subject of consciousness is a manifestation of mind and the object or objectified experience of the ball of light is an expression of mind as well.

We can meditate that inside the body at the heart level there is a ball of light the size of an egg. It is completely spherical, brilliant white in color, transparent, three-dimensional in form, made of light, and lacking solidity. We conceive of this sphere of light being present in the heart region and let the mind rest on this radiant ball.

Inevitably, other thoughts and distractions will arise in the mind. However, from the point of view of the meditation, these are distractions and we simply chop them off and return to the experience of the glowing white ball of light in the heart.

These distracting thoughts in the mind indicate that meditation is actually taking place. The first signpost in the development of shamatha is traditionally recognized to be this experience of thoughts cascading like a rushing mountain stream. We are becoming aware of all of the activity of the mind. Gradually, as we develop the shamatha approach and instill stability and tranquility of mind, these thoughts, emotions and distractions begin to diminish.

The experience of the second stage of shamatha will be that of a slowly flowing stream. There will still be a sense of activity of the mind but it will be much more controlled and cohesive. Unfortunately, many people have difficulty through the first stage. When they become aware of all of the activity in the mind, they take it as a sign that the practice is somehow wrong, that either there is no blessing in the practice of dharma or that they themselves are incompetent as meditators. The problem is not that the practice is without benefit or blessing, or that we are hopeless meditators. It is that there are very solid levels of confusion and obscuration in the mind. Fundamental ignorance, dualistic clinging, emotional confusion and karma have been reinforced in an infinite process. In particular, dualistic clinging and emotional confusion play great parts in the mental agitation that we experience while we meditate.

This is an indication that we are going to need to exert ourselves. It will take effort, diligence and commitment to the practice. It will also take a sincere effort to purify ourselves of these obscurations and negativity and to develop our positive qualities of merit and deepening awareness, for the practice to be successful. Traditionally, the teachings assert that it is not so much meditation as acclimatization. By familiarizing ourselves with the experience of meditation, our experience is actually transformed. It becomes a spacious realm of awareness. Meditation is something that we learn. We become accustomed to experiencing in a new way through meditation. This culminates in the spontaneous experience of spacious awareness.

Therefore, meditation is very much based on habitual practice, acclimatizing ourselves to a particular way of experiencing which is compared to the experience of a vast body of water without a ripple on the surface. There comes a feeling of bliss, not ultimate bliss, which cannot be limited or exhausted, but certainly a kind of physical and mental well-being beyond anything we have experienced before. It is beyond what we can express in our mundane frame of reference. This practice is also the basis for various psychic powers, such as clairvoyance, which may arise as the practice becomes more well-established.

If we do not receive any guidance from qualified teachers at this point, either because we lack contact with teachers or because we lack the ability to implement the teachings, we may find ourselves in a cul-de-sac. We may wish to spend our life in the cultivation of this blissful, stable, peaceful state of mind. However, that is an error from the point of view of spiritual practice, because while it leads to superior states of rebirth within the cycle of samsara, it does not represent a supreme path to enlightenment. It cannot liberate the mind and allow the mind to transcend limitations which bring about rebirth in this cycle of conditioned existence. No doubt it was this situation that Milarepa described when he said, "Without clinging to the deep pool of shamatha, allow the flower of vipasyana to bloom." The poetic example that he was presenting was that of a deep, still pool of water in which we can get so lost that any future growth is impossible. We would be like a water lily remaining dormant at the bottom of the pool without actually extending its stem to the surface to bloom. It is not enough to have developed tranquility of mind; we have to allow true insight to blossom.

The practice of meditation in spiritual development is one of gaining greater freedom of mind and control over our own experience. This begins with shamatha, the ability of mind to rest without distraction. Once that has been established as a basis, any approach that we use, such as developing further insight, instilling a particular aspect of our experience such as compassion or emptiness, or using the tantric techniques of creation and fulfillment, is going to be more fruitful. What is needed, then, is something which will produce not only the freedom of mind to stabilize itself, but also to extend that freedom of mind throughout every aspect of our experience. We will need a technique that will accomplish this rapidly and effectively, because, while we may be motivated to practice meditation, we have very little time to do so.

One effective technique extends the earlier example of the sphere of light meditation. We mentally orient ourselves so that the direction we face is east, regardless of what our actual physical orientation is. From the point of view of the practice, the direction in front of us is east. We meditate that there is a sphere, similar to the one we have visualized in our hearts, a very long distance in front of us. It is hundreds, thousands, millions of miles to the east of us. We rest the mind on the experience of that sphere of light far to the east. If the mind were something fixed and limited, then to force the mind to go all that distance to the east would be very problematic, but we are not limited by any such consideration. Our mind has perfect freedom to extend itself that far or further, to extend itself anywhere.

At this point, we shift our attention to the west, that is to say, behind us, and visualize that there is a sphere of light thousands and tens of thousands of miles away. We let the mind rest on the experience of that sphere far to the west.

Then we shift the focus of our awareness to the southern direction, which is to our right, and meditate that a sphere of white light is thousands and tens of thousands of miles away, and we let the mind rest on the experience. Finally, we shift the focus of our awareness to the north, which is to our left, conceiving of this white globe of light at the same vast distance, and we let the mind rest undistracted on that experience.

The next step is to conceive of all four spheres in all four directions simultaneously, along with the original sphere in the center of our heart, and let the mind rest on this simultaneous experience. The initial benefit of the mind resting upon a particular chosen experience undercuts our naive assumption that the mind is contained within the physical body, fixed and immovable.

What we find, in fact, is that the nature of mind has nothing to do with the body at all. This empty, luminous and unimpeded state of awareness, this nature of mind itself, is free to express itself in any way. This is not only true for four directions and a central point simultaneously, but we could also meditate in a hundred or million directions at once. Our fixation on self or ego severely limits the ability of the mind to express itself. It is like a very tight bond around the mind. This kind of approach, without posing any threat or harm to the mind, gradually loosens the bond and the mind becomes free to express itself.

The second benefit is very practical. It is very difficult to choose a single thing and meditate on it uniquely. Meditating on the globe in the heart without distraction is very often more than the beginner is able to do. By moving the focus of awareness around, we give a certain sense of openness to the meditation. When we become a little bit strained in one approach, we simply shift our attention to another direction. This gives the mind more play and some relief from holding the mind in a single place. At the same time, we do not lose the benefits of shamatha which this approach instills. Because this practice of meditation brings greater freedom and control of mind, inevitably we come to a significant stage of advanced realization, perhaps to first level Bodhisattvahood.

At that point, the mind is perfectly capable of maintaining one hundred states of meditative absorption in a single instant without there being any contradiction or conflict in the mind at all. It is also capable of manifesting as one hundred emanations in a single instant, of obtaining enlightenment or liberation through one hundred different pure realms of experience, of working directly for the benefit of one hundred beings in a single instant and so forth. All of these qualities and that power of mind come about through this technique of meditation.

QUESTIONS

You recommend that we use the organ of hearing to realize that mundane sounds are the union of sound and emptiness. Is there any connection between this experience and that of mantra as the union of sound and emptiness?

There is a connection in the sense that all sound is empty, regardless of whether it is the sound of mantra being recited or the sound of one of the elements in the environment. Regardless of the source of the sound, it is empty. However, we don't normally experience things in that way. We are very convinced that sound is in fact sound, very real, and when we hear a particular sound we think of it as a thing in and of itself. We ascribe agreeable qualities to some sounds, disagreeable ones to others. It has the power to play a great role in our lives to either benefit us or harm us because we pay so much attention to it and endow it with solidity.

The specific approach of shamatha meditation is to pay attention to sound as sound, beyond ascribing any characteristic to it at all, including emptiness. The point is to bring the mind to rest. This is as convenient as any other approach. We take a sensory experience like sound and use it as a quality in our experience which can be the basis for developing shamatha.

The deity meditation may also be utilized to instill this shamatha tranquility and stability of mind. We visualize the form of the divinity and rest the mind on that experience. If we find that the mind wanders from the divinity or we are not able to clearly visualize, it can be an equally effective method to recite the sound of the mantra and to rest in the sound of the mantra as sound. The sound of our own recitation of the mantra provides the basis or support for developing shamatha experience. Whether we are using the sound of the elements, an external sound, or whether we are using our own generation of the sound of the mantra as sound for the basis of shamatha, it is equally effective.

The point is, of course, that as sentient beings, as unenlightened beings in the cycle of rebirth, our biggest flaw is that the way we go about experiencing things is with this absolute conviction that what we experience is ultimately real. We are convinced that this body is absolutely real, so suffering, illness and pain arise from this conviction. The same thing can be said for speech, which is one aspect of sound; we are convinced that speech is something absolutely real. When we say words, we take the experience of hearing those words, that sound, as something real in and of itself. Benefit and harm arise from this conviction. We can be injured by words, damaged, hurt and upset, because we treat them as something absolutely real. The same thing can be said on the level of mind. All of the thoughts and emotions that come up in the mind are regarded as something real in and of themselves.

This naive assumption is relevant not only during our waking state of existence, but also takes place during the dream state when the mind projects all kinds of things which are experienced as though they were ultimately real, and during the Bardo or after-death experience, when there is a mere mental embodiment without there being any physical basis for the consciousness.

In the practice of Vajrayana, if we are to effect the transformation from unenlightened to enlightened being as rapidly as possible, ideally in a single lifetime, we will work on all these levels. We will transform this ordinary, naive experience of form as something solid and ultimately real in and of itself, into the experience of the emptiness of form. We will transform the ordinary naive experience of sound as sound into the experience of sound as sound and emptiness simultaneously. We will transform the experience of thoughts and emotions and mental activity into the experience of the union of emptiness and intelligent awareness. If we can effect transformation on those levels, we are powerless to prevent the attaining of enlightenment.

The purpose of Vajrayana deity meditation is to change or shift the focus of our attachment. We are presently convinced of the reality of our physical body and we are very attached to that concept. In deity meditation, we trade our own identity for an identification with the form of the divinity. We experience, for example, the thought, "I am no longer this physical body; I am Chenrezig." We become one with the divinity and identify with this form of the divinity which is approached as the union of form and emptiness. We trade our fixation on ordinary sound and speech for that of appreciating all sound as intrinsically the sound of the mantra, for example, *OM MANI PADME HUNG*, which is the experience of sound and emptiness simultaneously. We exchange our approach to mental activity by appreciating the thoughts, emotions and concepts which arise in the mind as the union of intelligent awareness and emptiness, the Mahamudra state of experience.

The Vajrayana practice tries to effect transformation on all these levels, physical, verbal and mental. Even if we are not able to effect this transformation in a single lifetime, the tendencies that we establish in this lifetime do not die with this physical body. Through an ongoing practice of meditation and the attempt to approach the experience of form as the experience of form and emptiness, the experience of sound as the experience of sound and emptiness, and the experience of mental activity as awareness and emptiness, we establish habitual tendencies that may manifest in the after-death state, when the physical body is no longer a limiting factor. It is possible for these tendencies to arise at any point during the after-death state and express themselves as transformation. The immediacy of the Bardo experience means that if those tendencies do arise and become part of our conscious experience, then this transformation can be effected instantaneously, because the physical body, which was a delaying factor, is no longer present. Then the experience of form as empty form, sound as empty sound, and thought and mental activity as empty awareness can take place instantaneously. This is another reason why the Vajrayana is a very rapid path. It provides an opportunity in the Bardo state if it is impossible for the practitioner to attain to the ideal of enlightenment in a single lifetime. The importance of the deity meditation such as the Chenrezig practice can hardly be overstated.

In addition to our own efforts, there is, in tantric practice, the blessing of the divinity and the blessing of the mantra; our own efforts are met with blessing, which creates a very powerful situation. We should not underestimate the powerful blessing of something like a mantra nor the power of our tendencies that develop through practice.

One of the principal students of the Buddha was an Arhat named Shariputra. This individual's mother was not interested in dharma practice at all, and lived a very worldly, very mundane life. Shariputra wished to help his mother, so what he thought up was the idea of hanging a doorbell above her door. It would ring every time someone opened or closed her door. He said to his mother, "From now on, we've got a new rule in the house. Every time you hear the bell ring, you have to say *OM MANI PADME HUNG.*" This went on for the rest of her life.

When she died her consciousness took rebirth in a hell realm due to some very negative karma that was part of her makeup, and while she was in this hell realm, there was a large cauldron in which the denizens of this particular realm were boiling the forms of many hell beings. As one of them was stirring the pot with a large iron spoon, it hit the spoon against the cauldron. She heard this sound and this hell being that had been Shariputra's mother immediately said, "*OM MANI PADME HUNG.*" She was immediately liberated from her hellish rebirth.

This story is something which bears investigation, because when we have accepted someone as our guru, the keynote of that relationship is our faith and devotion to the guru and our conviction that the guru is, for us, Buddha. Now, Buddha is everywhere. The enlightened state of mind is not something which is localized. Enlightenment is the experience of the fundamental nature of mind itself, which is omnipresent, all-pervading, and not limited or hindered or localized in any way. Whether we receive blessing or not depends upon whether we have faith and devotion. That is the single quality which opens us to receiving blessing.

We can compare the source of blessing, which is our guru, the Buddha for us, to the moon rising in the sky at night. Wherever there is water on the earth, there will be a reflection of that moon regardless of how many surfaces of water there are; wherever there is someone with faith, that person will receive blessing. It does not matter at all whether our guru is alive or physically present. This is something that the sage Milarepa addressed when he said, "I will not take rebirth here; my consciousness will go to the realm of manifest joy in the eastern direction. In the future, whenever anyone prays to me with faith and devotion, I will be there and I will give them blessing."

Each teacher, in accordance with their qualities and abilities, does their very best to fulfill the role of spiritual advisor. In placing lamas in the centers that I have established in the West, I have hoped very much that through providing someone with experience, I can provide a source of advice, guidance and information that will help each student in their practice. These lamas can provide the teachings to people who are sincerely seeking this path to liberation, as can every qualified lama throughout the world.

If we approach any lama as our root guru and we have the faith and devotion appropriate in that context, we will receive blessing. The lama can also be regarded as an emanation of His Holiness the Karmapa or myself or any other teacher. Our own attitude will determine the particular blessing or the degree to which we will receive blessing from that relationship. The texts are quite specific. If the student considers the teacher to be the embodiment of all the Buddhas of the three times, the blessings of the Buddhas of the three times can be transmitted to that student through the agency of that teacher. It is dependent upon the student's own attitude the degree to which that student will receive blessing and benefit from the relationship with any teacher. Perhaps we could find many flaws in the guru's understanding or realization if we were an objective observer being critical in the situation, but if the student has faith, then that opening of the student's mind permits the student to receive blessing from the relationship.

To illustrate this there is a story about the Buddhist university Nalanda in India. During the course of this university's existence it was noted for the excellence of its standards and the diligence with which the scholars and pandits within that university studied and understood the Buddhist teachings. At a certain point there was an old monk in the monastery who was quite lazy and didn't wish to study at all.

The king of that area was a sponsor of the university and every month on the full moon day, he would request teaching from one of the members of the university. A throne would be erected and the person who had been selected by the group would mount the throne and the king and his people would take teaching. At one time, the members of the university decided to play a little trick on the lazy monk, so they appointed him to be the lecturer for the king's visit the next month. When the time came, the old monk was informed that it was his turn to mount the throne and despite his protests, he was put up there on the throne, in front of the king who was very respectfully waiting for the teaching that would be given.

Of course, this poor old fellow did not know a thing and he sat there and tried to think of something to say. The only thing he could think to say was, "You know, it really hurts me so much, it is so much suffering to be so dumb at this time, to not know a thing." Then he got down off the throne and that seemed to be the teaching. The king was sitting there very respectfully and all that he had heard was this one sentence. But because he had come into the situation with faith and confidence that he would receive something, he thought about it and said, "Well, there must have been some deep import to what this old teacher was saying."

The king took it home and reflected on it. He came to the understanding that not knowing anything was fundamental ignorance and that it was the cause of all suffering. The more he thought about it, the more he understood that the root of all suffering in human existence was fundamental ignorance of the nature of mind and the more he meditated upon that, the more the fundamental ignorance in his mind began to transform itself into direct experience and awareness. The king actually attained liberation from the teaching that he received from this old monk.

If there is no faith and devotion in the student's mind, then it does not matter whether there is a guru present or not; we are not open to the blessing and we would get as much benefit from being in a guru's presence as by calling a wild animal our guru.

Which aspect of our being is utilized in the process of identifying with divinities? If we find the formless meditation of emptiness quite satisfying in and of itself, how do we relate to the form of the divinity?

To begin with, if we are actually meditating upon emptiness, that alone is fine. We need not feel that somehow it is not a worthy practice. It is in fact the essence of all meditation because shunyata, emptiness, is the heart of all experience. If we are able to understand shunyata and meditate authentically in that state of emptiness, then no more would be required.

However, we may not be able to generate a true experience of emptiness. We may feel, "This is emptiness," but we are really experiencing a kind of dullness or stupidity in the mind. The mind is blank and it seems as if there is nothing happening in the mind. In fact, there is nothing happening in the mind. We take that to be emptiness when, in fact, it is a subtle form of stupidity which we are reinforcing through meditation. We have to guard against this.

As to the practical question of visualizing the form of the divinity, I do not see that this need pose much of a problem. If there is someone that we hate, it is very easy to have a perfectly clear impression of that person in our mind. If there is someone toward whom we are intensely attracted sexually, it is easy to have a clear impression of that person in our mind. Therefore, I do not see any problem in clearly visualizing the form of a divinity. It certainly is well within the power of mind to create a clear image of the divinity. We have no trouble thinking, "I am," so it should not be any problem thinking, "I am Chenrezig." It is simply a shift of focus in terms of what we are thinking that we are.

We are using the deeply rooted clinging that we have to *I am* to properly approach yidam meditation, during which we transplant the fixation from our usual conception of self to the form of the divinity. This is a shift in focus or shift in emphasis, like the old saying that to get water out of your ear, you pour more water into it and let it all flow out. In order to overcome ego clinging, we use ego clinging.

Would you please explain the ten levels of Bodhisattvahood, the ten bhumis?

The first level or *bhumi* of bodhisattva realization is the stage in which the individual has the direct experience, on an ongoing basis, of the nature of mind as empty, clear, and unimpeded. After this recognition ceases to be a temporary experience and becomes a stable element, be it ever so slight, that is the first bhumi. It is the first significant attainment of real freedom of mind and control over our experience. As such, it entails certain qualities which are indicative of the fact that some freedom of the mind has been achieved. Whereas now we are able to experience states of mental experience one at a time, the mind of the first level bodhisattva is able to experience one hundred simultaneous states of meditative absorption in a single instant, and experience no contradiction. The texts speak of twelve such qualities, which are termed the twelve hundreds. Some examples of these hundreds are the ability of the mind to manifest one hundred emanations in different realms of experience in a single instant to benefit other beings; the ability of the mind to meet with one hundred Buddhas in a single instant; the ability to experience one hundred pure realms in a single instant; the ability to recall one hundred previous existences and the ability to foresee the circumstances surrounding the next one hundred births. There are twelve such qualities which are traditionally noted as characteristic of this first level of freedom of mind and control over experience.

Developing from the first through the tenth bhumi and beyond this to complete enlightenment, our efforts in purification and development, which are technically termed the accumulation of merit, and our efforts in meditation, which are technically termed the accumulation of wisdom, become more mature. The stability developed in the first bhumi becomes more a part of our experience and the negative aspects of our being become more subtle and diminish. This is coupled with the elimination of the limiting and hindering factors that had previously prevented that experience from unfolding.

A comparison might be made to the waxing moon. The third day of the lunar month, there is a tiny crescent moon which can be compared to the first bhumi. The progression toward enlightenment is like the waxing of the moon until it is full. As a sign of this process, qualities that were experienced as elements of the first bhumi are augmented. The scope of the freedom of mind expands. The texts say that the twelve hundreds increase tenfold from the first to the second bhumi, tenfold again from second to third, and so forth, so that by the time we have experienced the tenth level of bodhisattva realization, we speak not of one hundred states of simultaneous samadhi in a single instant, but of ten million states in a single instant. We speak not of one hundred emanations but of ten million emanations, not of one hundred previous or future existences, but of ten million previous or future existences. The scope is expanded because the freedom of mind to express itself has increased with the elimination of the negative and hindering factors which had previously prevented that expression.

All the levels of confusion and obscuration that we now experience, fundamental ignorance, dualistic clinging, emotional confusion, and karmic tendencies, have both gross and subtle aspects. The first bhumi entails the complete elimination of the grosser aspects of the karmic veils of the mind, which is the most gross of the four levels of confusion. The seventh level bodhisattva realization entails the elimination of the grosser aspects of emotional confusion. With the attainment of eighth level, the grosser aspects of dualistic clinging are eliminated; and with the ninth and tenth levels, the subtler aspects are eliminated.

By the time we have attained to the tenth level of bodhisattva realization, the only factor still hindering or limiting the mind is an extremely subtle aspect of fundamental ignorance. This must be eliminated to attain complete enlightenment. The Tibetan term *sangye* defines Buddhahood, complete enlightenment, as the absolute elimination of every level of obscuration and hindering factors, and, therefore, the total manifestation of the inherent potential of mind.

What is the connection between shamatha and yidam meditation? The shamatha approach seems simple compared to yidam meditation. Should we extensively practice shamatha before embarking on yidam meditation?

Shamatha means simply the instilling of an experience of tranquility and stability in the mind. Shamatha techniques can take many different forms. We can develop shamatha through meditating on a statue of the Buddha. We can also develop shamatha by meditating upon the form of the divinity, the yidam, and in fact, this meditation is recommended as perhaps the most effective approach for developing shamatha. This is because it takes into account not only the personal efforts of the meditator but the blessing inherent in the form of the divinity and in the mantra that we are reciting. Our own efforts are augmented by the blessing inherent in the practice and this produces effects more profoundly and rapidly.

It is true that on a practical level people find it more approachable to use a less complicated technique such as meditating on a ball of light rather than on the more complex form of a divinity. From the point of view of practical convenience, then, a simplified approach is preferable; from the point of effectiveness, yidam meditation is preferable for developing shamatha.

Normally, we think of the sense organs as passive receptors of sensory stimuli rather than being active agents through which the mind is expressed. Could Rinpoche comment on the distinction?

In a sense we are looking at the same situation from two different angles. Either stimuli are being brought in or the mind is expressing itself outwardly. However, from an experiential point of view, it is more accurate to say that the mind is leaking out rather than something is seeping in. When we refer to our present state of existence, tradition speaks of the skandha of leakage. The skandha is a heap or pile of our experience which is literally termed leakage because the mind is leaking out of the sense organs. Rather than being a passive receptor for stimuli making their presence felt, the mind goes out to meet the object and in doing so, it leaks out of the sense organ to appreciate the object. The object is only one of the elements necessary for a perceptual situation to occur. Along with the object or stimulus, there must be the organ of sensing and the mind itself.

CHAPTER ELEVEN

SHAMATHA PRACTICE: OBJECTLESS MEDITATION

We have been discussing the luminosity and dynamic unimpeded quality of mind. Its nature is the luminous potential to know and its manifestation is unimpeded or unobstructed awareness. These are fundamental qualities of the nature of mind, but they are not something in themselves. They remain essentially empty and so the essential emptiness of mind is reflected in the fact that its luminosity and its dynamism are not solid, limited, fixed things. This is something which is crucial to understand and something that a spiritual teacher of meditation must convey to the student although only a small number of people are sensitive enough to immediately perceive what is being said and have some experience of it.

It is necessary for the student to reflect upon and understand these ideas, whether they use an analytical approach of dissecting their experience, or a more intuitive uncontrived approach. In meditation, we are letting the mind rest in its own nature without any artifice, allowing that experience to grow, and then at other times we are pursuing a train of thought, analyzing and dissecting our experience to come to some understanding of the nature of mind. This is how the student perceives that what the teacher has been saying is true. It is necessary for us to work through our own experience. Once we have had the experience of the empty, clear and unimpeded nature of mind itself, then there follows the experience that all the contents of mind are merely expressions of mind-nature rather than something in and of themselves.

If all thought and emotion and mental activity are merely expressions of mind and partake of mind-nature without being anything independent of mind, then when an emotion such as attraction arises in the mind, it is perceived for what it is, merely a manifestation of that empty, clear, and unimpeded mind-nature. There is no need to ascribe to that emotion of desire any reality in and of itself. There is no need to posit this emotion as something other than an empty manifestation of an empty mind. We are free from the necessity of being dominated by our emotions, whereas currently, we experience these emotions that arise in the mind as something very solid and real. Because we ascribe this solidity and reality to the emotion, we have no choice but to follow the dictates of that emotion; we have placed ourselves in a position where our feelings rule our activities. Once we have appreciated that the mind is empty, and that therefore all thought and emotion arising in the mind are empty, then we appreciate that any thought or passion is equally empty. It partakes of the essential emptiness of the mind from which it arises and is not any thing in and of itself, and certainly nothing solid or inflexible.

When, for example, a thought of passion or desire arises in the mind, if we have understood the emptiness of that emotion, then, as the emotion arises, we experience its intangibility, its empty essence, and spontaneously there arises the experience of bliss and emptiness. There is no need for us to abandon that particular emotion; there is no need for us to repress or suppress that emotion; there is no need for us to indulge in that emotion. We simply experience directly the essence of that thought or emotion, allowing it to liberate itself and express itself as an experience rather than as a conflicting emotion. This is a simultaneous experience of bliss and emptiness. With this very efficacious approach, the thought is liberated as it arises in the mind.

When a person experiences very strong anger or aggression, an intense hatred for someone to the point where he or she may actually want to hurt or to kill someone, if that person can use this approach, being aware of the emptiness of mind and experiencing thought and emotion that arise from the mind as mere manifestations of that mind-nature then, what will take place, rather than the ordinary experience of anger or hatred, is an experience of clarity and emptiness. We are not forced to deal with the emotion by suppressing it or manipulating it or indulging in it, but we can allow the clarity and sharpness which is inherent in that anger to express itself. This approach is very straightforward, very simple. We allow what was normally experienced as a conflicting emotion to arise as an experience.

Let us take the example of stupidity, the dullness or lethargy of mind which we all experience frequently throughout the day and also at night when there is no conscious activity in the mind at all. To experience that emotion of stupidity or mental apathy or dullness for what it is, to appreciate its emptiness, is to discover a fundamental transformation of unknowing to awareness. This intelligent or dynamic awareness, termed *rigpa* (rig.pa) in Tibetan, is experienced as essentially empty. Where once there was dullness, torpor and stupidity of mind, there is now a simultaneous experience of intelligent awareness and emptiness. We do not need to suppress this dullness of mind, nor do we have to indulge in it. We can use this approach to discover a very beneficial experience within what was normally experienced as a conflicting emotion.

Suffering and pain are unavoidable. They are part of being alive. Part of the human condition is that each and every human being must experience the pains of birth, aging, illness and disease, and death. This is something we cannot avoid. Our particular state of illusion as human beings follows that pattern of suffering and there is nothing we can do about it. In a country like America, however, we find such a high standard of living that most of the material needs of a human being have been answered. Excepting the limitations of the four great sufferings of birth, aging, sickness, and death, nearly everything else has been provided on a material level. However, there is still much mental suffering. In fact, the principal source of suffering in the West is mental in nature. Westerners suffer particularly from the emotional imbalance, unhappiness and confusion that all beings experience, because there is no consideration given to dealing skillfully with emotions. In not understanding the essential emptiness of mind and the essential emptiness of the emotions, we find ourselves very much subject to emotional conflict.

The three patterns of attachment, aversion, and stupidity are primary emotions which give rise to many other complicated emotional situations as they interact with one another. Due to a lack of awareness of what is actually taking place when the mind experiences an emotion, people suffer from their emotions. This approach of understanding the nature of mind to see into the nature of emotionality is the single most effective method for dealing with emotional pain and suffering; it frees us from the laborious process of having to manipulate or transform or play with the emotions in any way. We experience the energy for what it is rather than what we had assumed it to be. There is no more simple, straightforward, or effective approach for dealing with emotional pain and suffering.

These days, one common approach to dealing with the emotions both on an ordinary level and on a therapeutic level seems to be the idea that the more we express one emotion, the less there will be of it. If we are angry people, the more we express our anger, the more skillfully we are dealing with it. Eventually the reservoir is going to run dry. If people have problems of sexual desire or attachment, then to act out those desires seems a skillful way of dealing with them. Perhaps for someone who has no inkling of the teachings of dharma, that is the only means they have; but from the point of view of the teachings of dharma, this is really an idiot's way of going about things, because the more we express emotions, the more emotions there are to be expressed. The more we express an emotion, the more we reinforce the tendency for that emotion to arise. By surrendering to an emotion when it arises, we are augmenting and embellishing and increasing it rather than exhausting it. The very fact that the emotions are empty means that they are inexhaustible. If the mind were something solid and real and tangible that gave rise to emotions which were solid and real and tangible, we could chip away at them until they were finished; but the mind is essentially empty and the emotions which arise from the mind are essentially empty and, therefore, they have no limit. They could be extended and developed as much as we chose to expand and develop them, because there is no way to exhaust that emotionality. The importance of seeing into the nature of mind is to see into the nature of the emotion rather than looking at its superficial content.

The Buddha once said that dealing with the emotions that we experience in this life is rather like dealing with thorns. If the whole earth were covered with thorns and we wanted to walk somewhere, we would have two choices. We could pick all the thorns out of our way, which is a very laborious process, or we could put on a pair of thick shoes. Likewise, in dealing with the emotions, we can employ a kind of hit and miss approach, dealing with each situation on a superficial level, or we can attempt to instill in ourselves some understanding of the nature of mind itself and the nature of emotionality. That would provide a kind of protection, allowing us to move through situations without any harm.

Perhaps you have had the experience of sitting at home where everything is comfortable and you are quite happy. Then, all of a sudden, you find yourself in a state of emotional imbalance, with some strong emotion arising in the mind and completely transforming your experience. You can no longer stand to be where you are. You are completely agitated and all you can think about is playing out that emotion.

If we are looking for a medicine to cure the disease of emotional imbalance, we are not going to find a better remedy than emptiness. Experiencing the emptiness of emotion is what liberates us from that need to recapture the balance of our lives, because we have not been knocked off balance by emotional upheavals in the first place. Contentment and well-being arise first and foremost from understanding the nature of mind and the nature of emotionality.

During the infinite process of rebirths that the mind has been experiencing to no ultimate purpose, there has been continual activity in the mind. Thoughts, emotions and experiences have arisen continuously, but none of these have any substance. If those thoughts and emotions had been solid, we would have to look somewhere to find where they had been stored. But it is all intangible and it has passed away. The emotions that we have experienced are not stored within the body, nor are they stored anywhere outside the body. They are not, ultimately speaking, anything real to which we need ascribe tangibility or solidity. They are essentially empty and intangible, expressions of the intangible and empty nature of mind. We can derive much benefit from understanding that and more from experiencing it.

Once we have experienced and appreciated the nature of mind, then the battle is half won, the task is half over, and the intention of the Buddha in presenting the dharma is half realized. We are significantly closer to enlightenment through that single experience, that single act of appreciating the nature of our mind. To approach this understanding, we need instruction.

In looking for the nature of mind, we have to be aware of our methods. No doubt there are many very brilliant scientists in the world nowadays who are looking for the mind, but, from the point of view of spiritual realization, what is looking for the mind is mind itself, and so it is a vicious circle. The subject is looking for the object which is the subject which is the object, and as long as mind keeps looking for itself in that intellectual or conceptual framework, it is not going to find itself. It is an endless search. This does not mean that we cannot use the intellect to approach the experience of the nature of mind itself. It is just that, in and of itself, it will not be ultimately effective.

There are two quite valid approaches in meditation, both of which are necessary, both of which are quite important. The first is an intellectual or analytical approach and the other is an intuitive, spontaneous approach. In the first case, we periodically receive teachings from a guru and then take them home and work with them. We contemplate what we have been given; we compare it to our own experience to validate it or invalidate it; we dissect or analyze our experience to attempt to discover the truth of what we have been taught on a conceptual level. This is going to be very beneficial, but it is not going to be ultimately fruitful in giving us the authentic experience of the nature of mind itself. That requires the second, more intuitive approach, which is seeing the nature of mind without looking for it. In contrast to an objectifying process of mind looking for itself, there is a simple state of dwelling in bare awareness, where the natural essence of mind is allowed to express itself.

Therefore, rather than looking for the mind, we experience the nature of mind in a direct way. There is no one looking and nothing is looked at; there is no subject or object, but simply the state of spontaneous awareness in which the nature of mind itself manifests. At this point, we are not looking at the mind as we were during the analytical meditation but rather we see without looking and experience without analyzing. Once there has been the fundamental experience of the nature of mind, then the other aspects of enlightened being to which we have made reference, the experience of speech and sound as the union of sound and emptiness, and the physical body as the union of form and emptiness and so forth, are not problematic at all. This is quite straightforward once we have grasped the significance of the fundamental experience of the nature of mind itself.

To begin a session of shamatha meditation, we take refuge and arouse bodhicitta, the ultimate and compassionate motivation. Next we align the physical posture of the body. One of the reasons why an erect, dignified posture for meditation is considered quite important is because this lends to the body a sense of balance. When the body is held straight, the subtle channels of energy in the body are not blocked or contorted in any way; everything can run smoothly. When energy flows freely in our body, there is a sense of stability and calm in the body and thus in the mind. At this point, at least, there is an intimate interconnection between mind and body, so to instill calm and tranquility of mind, physical posture is quite important.

If we are pursuing a formless or objectless approach in shamatha, then the experience of formless awareness, of emptiness, becomes the approach for developing tranquility and stability of mind. Ideally, of course, from the point of view of Mahamudra realization, our experience of emptiness is completely nonconceptual. It is beyond any kind of mental construct as to what emptiness is, but is merely the direct experience of the intangibility of mind. This is not something we are likely to be capable of experiencing at the beginning, and so our approach will of necessity be involved with these kinds of mental constructs. This is unavoidable and, in fact, is quite appropriate from the point of view of meditation. Even though the nature of mind itself is inherently intangible and empty at this stage, we focus the mind on the experience of emptiness. There is a sense of objectifying or directing the mind toward that experience of emptiness to the exclusion of other thoughts or concepts which would be distractions at this point.

In this approach, then, the focus of the mind is the experience of the essential nature of mind as intangible, as spacious, as free from any limitation; it has no circumference, no parameters, no color or form, no shape or size or location at all. The point is to remain in that state without distraction. When thoughts and distractions arise in the mind, we should remain true to the experience of the essential emptiness of mind without following after or indulging in the thoughts or concepts that present themselves.

We should begin this kind of approach by employing it only for very short periods of time, that is, no more than five or ten minutes, according to the traditional texts. Unless we are acclimatized to this alert and clear state of formless awareness, pursuing it for very long will lead to the clarity and alertness of the mind becoming dimmed and a certain dullness or torpor of mind setting in. This may go unnoticed by the meditator and then our efforts at developing shamatha become polluted.

Whether we use a shamatha approach to develop tranquility and stability of mind, or a vipasyana approach to develop insight into the nature of mind, our wisdom is utilized on three levels. The first kind of wisdom is an intellectual one which is developed through hearing teachings, studying them, and understanding them on a conceptual

level. The second kind of wisdom is developed through contemplation, by taking the teachings that we have been given, and reflecting
on them again and again, validating them against our own experience
so that we come to a deeper understanding. Finally, there is meditative wisdom, in which intellectual or conceptual wisdom becomes
experiential and completely intuitive by allowing the mind to rest in
an uncontrived state in which wisdom arises as direct experience. In
order to successfully follow any chosen path in meditation, it is necessary for us to develop our wisdom on these three levels.

QUESTIONS

What is the relationship between the physical body and the mind?

Our being is both mental and physical in nature. If there were merely
a physical body without a mind, then all we would have would be a
corpse. We could not speak of emptiness, clarity, and unimpeded-ness,
because we would be speaking about a corpse. A corpse cannot think;
a corpse cannot see things; it cannot feel or taste or touch or smell
things. A corpse is inanimate matter, because it is not imbued with the
consciousness which experiences everything. Only when the physical
body is animated by a consciousness can the physical body be the
vehicle by which the mind's empty, clear, and unimpeded nature express itself. It experiences form by seeing sights, hearing sounds, smelling smells, tasting tastes, touching textures, thinking thoughts. It is
only when there is the animate quality of the empty, clear, and unimpeded state of awareness that is mind, that the body comes into the
picture at all.

The idea that we are doing something, are meditating, is not such a
bad thing. Actually, it is quite important. We have no choice but to go
about our spiritual practice in the way that we are accustomed to going about things, which is saying to ourselves, "I am going to do this."
It might as well be, "I am going to do spiritual practice." Eventually, if
we do exert ourselves and stay with the practice sincerely, the function of the practice will allow dualistic clinging to exhaust itself, but it
is rather like the growth of a flower. We cannot expect to plant the
seed and immediately have a blooming flower. First a sprout arises,
then it sends out leaves and shoots and eventually we have a flower.
To expect it all to happen instantaneously is unrealistic. It will take
time; it will take some effort; but we should not doubt that it will take
place. The important thing is not to doubt. We keep to the practice
with the understanding that it will be effective and that the flower

will blossom; gradually, dualistic clinging will exhaust itself. We will come to a more spontaneous place where the meditation occurs.

Generally, attachment to clinging and egocentricity are considered to be a real fetter, chaining us to the cycle of rebirth; if they were not there in the first place, we would begin liberating ourselves from that cycle of rebirth. First and foremost, we are practicing in order to liberate ourselves. We are thinking, "I want to liberate myself from the cycle of rebirth. I want to practice dharma. I want to get enlightened." It is a selfish point of view. We are concerned with doing something ourselves, which is not bad, because it means that we do actually start. As we begin to approach enlightenment, this fettering effect of ego clinging and preoccupation with the self becomes less and less of a problem. It dissipates itself as a natural result of the experience and realization which is unfolding.

Suppose you want to go to India. You would not think, "I want to go to India," with the thought that you will never get there. You think, "I want to go to India," because you assume or you hope that at some time in the future, you will actually arrive. You get your tickets, collect your baggage, get visas and passports, and then you board the airplane. The only reason you get on that plane is because you once said to yourself, "I want to go to India." As the plane is flying to India, you are not so concerned with getting to India, because you are almost there. By the time you land at the airport in India, you are not concerned at all with getting to India, because you have arrived. Likewise by the time we have attained enlightenment, there is no longer any need to think, "I want to become enlightened," because we are almost there. We are going to get there. At a certain point, we know we are going to get there and the question of whether or not I am involved becomes less and less of a factor.

During the Chenrezig meditation, there is a formless period of meditation. If someone finds it difficult to maintain this state of empty awareness for a long period of time, can they alternate the form and formless, the object and objectless meditation?

Since the main purpose of meditation is to benefit the mind, we are interested in an approach which facilitates the meditator being able to feel comfortable with the technique. Therefore, we could adopt the approach you suggest, balancing the object and objectless meditation techniques, in the following way. After the recitation of the mantra, when we are visualizing the form of the divinity in Chenrezig meditation, there is a process of dissolution whereby the visualization is condensed into a tiny point of light which we then meditate as dissolving into nothingness and we let the mind rest in an empty state of formless awareness. This dissolution process is very effective for introducing the mind to the experience of emptiness. We should, ideally, remain resting in that state of empty awareness as long as is comfortable. However, if we find that the mind is unable to maintain that approach without dullness or distraction, we could call to mind the ball of light that was the last form in the meditation, and rest the mind on that for as long as is comfortable. The dissolution and reincorporation could be alternated as needed.

What you say is quite true. When we are beginning in meditation, it is very difficult for the mind to rest in any given state. Another approach that we might find very effective, if we are using the Chenrezig meditation, is to prolong the dissolution process of the visualization. The way the dissolution is normally described is that we are conceiving of ourselves in the form of the divinity, the bodhisattva; we are conceiving of all beings as the bodhisattva and the entire external environment as the realm of pure experience. First, we visualize that the external realm and the beings in that realm dissolve into light and this light is absorbed into our own form as the divinity. Then our form as the divinity dissolves and is absorbed into the mantra and seed syllable that we are visualizing in our heart. Next, the letters of the mantra dissolve into the central seed syllable and then the seed syllable dissolves from the bottom upward and we are left with a tiny point of light as the last stages of the visualization.

What we could do is prolong the process so that we spend perhaps five minutes on each stage of the visualization. First, we meditate the entire external realm dissolving into light and being absorbed into our own form as Chenrezig, the bodhisattva of compassion, and rest at that point of the visualization for five minutes. Then, we visualize our form as the divinity slowly dissolving into the syllables in the heart and let the mind rest on that for five minutes. Each stage of the dissolution can be followed by resting in it for five minutes, so that by the time we are left with the tiny point of light, the mind is very acclimatized to the dissolving of the form. The actual entrance of the mind into the state of emptiness is less of a shock than when we dissolve the form very quickly.

This particular technique of dissolving the visualization, which forms a bridge between the form and the formless aspects of the meditation, is a particular keynote of the tantric approach. The bridge between form and formless can be experienced in many ways depending upon the acumen of the practitioner. Ultimately, we will not experience a gap between form and formless. At that time, if we meditate on a form, we will experience the formless, because we will not experience form as solid form but as empty form, the union of form and emptiness. The form and formless will be simultaneously present and a stage of dissolution, acting as a bridge from one to the other, is not necessary.

However, even for someone with less developed capabilities, the bridge can be effected very quickly. Such a person can employ a particular technique in which we are meditating on a given form. For example, we see ourselves as the divinity and all beings as the divinity and the entire outer realm as the realm of pure experience. Then instantly we dissolve the form of the visualization and are in a state of formlessness. In this technique, there is a gap. There is a difference between one state and the other, but the change from one to the other can be effected very quickly, very smoothly. Obviously, for someone who is beginning to practice, that kind of dexterity of mind is not going to be forthcoming right away, so the gradual dissolution is one very profound technique in tantra for acclimatizing the mind to passing from one state of experience to another, from a form to a formless state.

Could you please discuss some means of dealing with distraction and dullness during shamatha? I am particularly concerned with agitation due to bodily tension.

When we are pursuing shamatha practice to instill tranquility and stability to the mind, the two obstacles to the meditation are dullness of mind and agitation of the mind, in which it becomes untameable and uncontrollable.

In the case of dullness or torpor setting in, we can do very practical things on a physical level, such as sitting straighter, or opening our eyes which wakes up the mind, or raising our eyes which lifts the consciousness. If we are using a form visualization, we can work with the visualization in a way that will remedy the situation. For example, if we are meditating on a sphere of light, and the mind is becoming dull, we can meditate that the ball of light shoots up into the air through the crown of our head like a shooting star, follow it up with the mind, position it far in the air above our heads and keep ourselves focused on it.

If the mind is too agitated, that may be an indication that we are too tense and should relax the posture or lower the eyes so that we are resting our gaze on the ground in front of us. We are attempting to bring the mind back down and ground it. If we are meditating on the ball of light in the heart, we can meditate that it becomes very heavy and begins to sink down to the ground and follow it with the mind in that direction. That will help to counterbalance the agitation of mind.

If we find that our distraction in meditation is largely due to physical discomfort because we have not trained enough in correct meditation posture to be able to sit comfortably, then we should take that into account. We do not need to strain to achieve some kind of correct posture if in fact it is causing the mind to be too tense.

A very famous Tibetan woman whose name was Machig Labkyi Drönma (Ma.gcig.Lab.kyi.sGron.ma) and who was the main figure in one of the principal lineages of Tibetan Buddhism, the Chöd (gCod) lineage, once said, "The quality of a mountain stream is determined by the force or the speed with which it rushes down the side of the mountain, crashing into rocks and bounding off rocks as it goes down, but the quality of a yogi's practice is determined by that yogi's poise." The more a mountain stream crashes against things as it pours down the mountain side, the more dramatic and inspiring it is; from the point of view of a yogi's practice, the poise in meditation of being able to balance oneself between too much tension and too much relaxation determines the quality of the meditator's practice. The great Mahasiddha Tilopa of India once said, "If tension can be relaxed, there is no doubt that liberation will occur."

After I still my mind's thoughts through shamatha, visual impressions of shapes and colors arise that are quite distracting. Sometimes they disappear and at other times they are quite persistent. Why is this happening?

This kind of experience would seem to be due to a subtle dullness of mind which creeps in during the initial phase of relative calm and tranquility of mind. While the mind is calm or tranquil, what is missing is a kind of alertness, a luminous or clear quality to the experience. Because there is the initial fault of subtle dullness, then these kinds of hallucinations tend to arise later as a consequence. The best thing to do is to stop the meditation for a short time, and then come back to the meditation, so that we are making a fresh start, rather than trying to push through it.

When we make an effort to generate the experience of meditation, don't we run into the danger of manufacturing it or of convincing ourselves that it is happening?

In order for meditation to become spontaneous, we first have to work at it. It is due to our efforts in meditation and the blessing of the practice itself that we gradually attain to that spontaneity where the experience of the nature of mind simply arises without work. However, to say that we should make efforts in meditation does not mean that we should think of it as creating an experience. We are simply appreciating what is already there. To experience anything at all, even in the limited way that we now experience things, requires that the mind have the qualities of emptiness, luminosity, and unimpededness. We do not have to create that experience of the nature of mind because it is here already. We are simply appreciating what is already taking place. The more effort we make in the particular technique that we are using in meditation, the more we come not only to appreciate the nature of mind on a conceptual level but also to experience it directly as something arises in the mind.

CHAPTER TWELVE

FOUR CAUSES LEADING TO REBIRTH IN DEWACHEN

There are four causes that bring the mind to rebirth in Dewachen, the realm of pure bliss, which is also known as Sukhavati in Sanskrit. The realm of Dewachen can be thought of as a high level Nirmanakaya pure realm or as a bridge to a low level of Sambhogakaya. This is a realm of experience equivalent to the first level of bodhisattva realization. This represents the state of being that transcends the limitations of the cycle of rebirth in that there is no need for the consciousness to take rebirth due to karmic circumstances. It is possible that, from the enlightened perspective, a being who has attained this level of realization may choose to consciously emanate in samsara for the purpose of helping other beings. However, this is a matter of choice, not karmic necessity.

Before our present world system came into being, there was a period of twenty intermediate kalpas of voidness following the destruction or disintegration of the last world system in this area of the universe. After this, there was a process of creation beginning with the consolidation of the various elements. The mandala of the wind element was followed by the mandala of the water element and so forth, gradually forming our physical universe. This process of creation, before any life took rebirth in this particular world system, was an additional twenty kalpas in duration. From the time that beings began to populate the various realms of this world system, until the appearance and passing of the thousandth Buddha, there will be a period of twenty kalpas. At this time, the karma which maintains this world system will exhaust itself. Then the process of dissolution and disintegration of the various elements and physical makeup of this universe will occur again. This will take twenty kalpas. These phases of voidness, creation, duration and destruction form a period of eighty kalpas, which is termed one mahakalpa, or great kalpa.

The Amitabha sutras describe Dewachen, the realm of pure being, as having come into being some ten days ago. It should be understood, however, that for the being experiencing Dewachen, one day is equivalent to one mahakalpa. It was that long ago that the aspirations of the Buddha Amitabha first gave rise to this realm of pure being.

When the mind comes into the experience of Dewachen, it is realizing the first bodhisattva bhumi. It is an experience that is quite extraordinary and aesthetic in its implications, because the mind takes rebirth in a miraculous way. It incarnates in the center of a lotus flower, which opens to expose a realm of paradisiacal beauty and contentment to the being experiencing that pure state.

Once having achieved the enlightened perspective of the first bodhisattva level, a being may employ the increased freedom of mind to manifest one hundred times in any instant in any realm for the purpose of benefitting other beings. It is also possible for a being to experience other pure realms and to encounter other Buddhas.

As far as other pure realms are concerned, some of these are very high Sambhogakaya pure form realms. In order for the mind to experience these realms, it is necessary to attain to the eighth level of bodhisattva realization. Even in the case of lower level Sambhogakaya pure realms, it is necessary for the being to experience at least first level bodhisattva realization. Lower level Nirmanakaya pure realms require a very scrupulous moral purity on the part of the practitioner and an incredible accumulation of merit.

Due to the aspirations of the Buddha Amitabha, the single crucial element in determining the ability of the mind to take rebirth in this state is the aspiration of the individual. All that is required is absolute conviction that this realm of experience is possible, and the fervent aspiration to attain to that state. The Amitabha sutras describe the particular characteristics of this pure realm as being attributable to the faith and confidence of the practitioner.

While it is aspiration and conviction that is the crucial factor in determining whether or not the mind can experience this realm of pure bliss, we need to consider the four factors or causes which are essential for the practice to be successful. The first of these is the supportive role played by our clear visualization of this pure environment. This is something which is not dramatically different from other Vajrayana practices. For example, when we are performing the Tara ritual, we are meditating the mandala of Green Tara surrounded by the twenty-one other forms of Tara in the sky before us. The frame of reference that we develop through our visualization, and the faith that this is actually present before us, is the same basic principle. In the case of the Dewachen practice, the particular content of the visualization is different. We visualize ourselves in the presence of Amitabha and the retinue of Buddhas and Bodhisattvas.* We conceive of our present environment as the pure realm of bliss. The external world of rocks, trees, water and mountains become much more precious, much more beautiful than the natural world as we experience it now. It is a completely perfect realm of experience, where the elements can never be the cause of any suffering or harm for the inhabitants.

We envision that at the center of this enormous environment is a jewel throne upon which is the form of the Buddha Amitabha, deep red in color and clad in the robes of a monk. He is seated in full meditation posture, holding an alms bowl in his lap, and surrounded by a vast assemblage of Buddhas, Bodhisattvas and Arhats. These figures form the retinue around the central figure of the mandala, Amitabha Buddha. The more clearly we can visualize this mandala, the better support it will be for our meditation and for the generation of our aspirations and prayers. The crucial factor is our conviction, regardless of whether we are capable of clearly visualizing this mandala. As is quite accurately and appropriately said in one of the texts of the Indian Buddhist tradition, all phenomenal experience is based upon our intention and aspiration; it is on that level that we can be supremely effective. If we develop the intention, aspiration and conviction that something is true, we have a greater chance to effect that transformation.

The second or causal factor of rebirth in Dewachen is our own purification and development. We accomplish this through eliminating the negative and obscuring elements of our being, developing and encouraging the positive aspects, developing our merit and deepening our awareness. This is similar to what we experience in our present life. If we have sufficient stock of merit due to virtuous karma, then we will be successful in whatever we do; if we do not have it, then regardless

---

*Editor's note: This visualization and the ensuing prayers may be found in the liturgy for the deity Amitabha.

of the efforts we make, there is no basis upon which prosperity or success can grow. We cannot expect to achieve results without developing these causal factors of merit and awareness.

However, in spiritual practice, the qualities which determine our success in establishing this basis of merit are somewhat different. The most important qualities are faith and confidence in our spiritual teacher, the Three Jewels and the spiritual principles from which we seek inspiration; our compassion and loving kindness for beings; and our wisdom in understanding that phenomenal existence is an expression of mind and that the mind itself is something essentially empty. If this faith, compassion and wisdom are present in abundance, then our spiritual development will be very effective.

The effort to purify ourselves of negativity and obscurations and to develop merit and awareness is encapsulated in the Seven Branches Prayer of the Mahayana. This prayer appears frequently in liturgical texts because it is one of the finest techniques for purification and development. The Seven Branches are, first, rendering homage to the sources of refuge, the Three Jewels and the Three Roots; second, making offerings; and third, confessing our negativity and obscurations. The confession is done not only in the context of this life, but of all the negativity that has been committed by ourselves and all beings in an infinite series of rebirths. We acknowledge and confess our own faults and shortcomings as well as those of others.

The fourth branch of this prayer is rejoicing in the merit and virtue of others, including that of ordinary and enlightened beings. The fifth branch is requesting our gurus, the Three Jewels, and the Buddhas and Bodhisattvas to continue to turn the wheel of the dharma by presenting teachings and making them accessible to beings in samsara. The sixth branch is appealing to the Buddhas, Bodhisattvas and spiritual teachers to continue to manifest in future kalpas until the cycle of rebirth may be emptied and all beings may attain enlightenment. We supplicate them so that the source of spiritual blessing and inspiration will not be lost. The final branch is dedicating the virtue and merit of the preceding six branches and all spiritual practice to the benefit of all beings. This prayer incorporates all of the elements for purifying negativity and developing merit and awareness.

The third cause that brings the mind to rebirth in Dewachen is the benefit that our practice receives from the fact that our motivation is an altruistic one. This is the time when our bodhicitta, the altruistic and compassionate concern for others, becomes very significant in spiritual practice. When we develop loving kindness and compassion, true bodhicitta, every action becomes far more significant. If we make an offering of a single candle on a shrine with a totally altruistic motivation, it is a far more meritorious act than another person without that motivation offering hundreds of thousands of candles. There is a concentrated or embellished quality to everything that we do when it springs from this altruistic motivation. Our aspirations are easier to realize if they are grounded in and arise from this selfless, compassionate concern for others.

When these three factors are present, it is the fourth factor, aspiration, which gives direction to the practice. For the mind to successfully attain the state of pure experience, there needs to be a strong aspiration. This is the deciding factor in the practice, once the basis has been formed by the other three elements. The aspiration, in this instance, is for ourselves and all beings to attain to the state of Dewachen. Even if we attain this state while other beings have not, we will continue to work for the benefit of others from that enlightened perspective. This is a commitment that we never forget. Our altruistic motivation is the stable foundation upon which we build our perception of the external environment as the realm of Dewachen.

Having laid the foundation of our bodhicitta, we envision the form of Amitabha Buddha in front of us; we have the conviction that we are actually in his presence and the motivation to experience the realm of Dewachen. In the liturgy, the context of the visualization is established by a long prayer of aspiration to experience Dewachen, which was composed by the famous Kagyupa lama, Karma Chagme Rinpoche (Kar.ma.Chags.med.Rin.po.che). It is a description of the pure realm in the presence of the Buddha Amitabha and the retinue of Buddhas and Bodhisattvas, and functions as the first factor, the support which is derived from our clear visualization.

The second factor is the causal factor of the development of our personal efforts at purification and development. This is done through the Seven Branches Prayer, which is extended in this liturgy because of the emphasis placed upon this element.

The next section of the liturgy concerns the attitude that we develop in physically choosing either continued existence in the cycle of rebirth or the ability to transcend that cycle and liberate our mind to experience a pure realm of bliss. There is an examination of the faults and limitations of samsaric existence, the instability and frustrating nature of existence in the cycle of rebirth, and the fact that nothing exists on that level that can be relied upon. This is a reinforcement of our aspiration to attain that experience of pure and stable bliss as opposed to continuing to wander in the confusion and suffering that fuels the cycle of rebirth.

The concluding section of the liturgy is a description of the experience of the state of pure bliss. The incredible longevity, the qualities of mind, the bliss of the mind, the ability of the mind to emanate in order to benefit other beings—all of these are examined in turn, to impress upon the mind the qualities of this state of existence and to further reinforce our aspiration to attain to it.

If our aspirations and prayers incorporate these four factors to insure the success of the practice, then we need not doubt whether the practice will be effective. We will undoubtedly attain this state of experience which is free from suffering and imbued with supreme bliss, and is the context from which we can be incredibly effective at working for the benefit of others.

CHAPTER THIRTEEN
MAHAMUDRA

The Mahamudra experience and approach is perhaps the quintessence of all Buddhadharma. In order for this quintessential approach to be effective, we must have some understanding of the nature of the mind that we are attempting to discover through the Mahamudra techniques.

Mahamudra has three aspects: foundation, path, and fruition. Foundation Mahamudra is the understanding which is based on our appreciation of the nature of mind. This must be augmented by the process of path Mahamudra which is direct experience and acclimatization to that nature of mind through meditation. Finally, there is the fruition or result aspect of Mahamudra, which is the actualization of the potential inherent in the nature of mind. This actual aspect of transcending awareness includes the Dharmakaya, Sambhogakaya, and Nirmanakaya as the facets of completely enlightened experience. It is not beneficial to speak of Mahamudra lightly; we must not ignore any of these three aspects of the Mahamudra approach.

Foundation Mahamudra implies a deep appreciation and understanding of the nature of mind. When we say that this is the correct view, we do not use that phrase in a casual sense. Very often, we say, "Well, in my view, such and such is the case," but this does not necessarily mean that we have understood it at all. We may say, "I believe in previous existences," or, "I don't believe in future existences," but very often our talk is not based on experience and appreciation, but merely on an idea to which we give lip service. What is meant in foundation

His Eminence Kalu Rinpoche
Photograph taken at Evam Choden Center, Kensington, California.
© *Mike Mokotoff*

Mahamudra is a thorough appreciation of the nature of mind itself, the mind with which we are working, and the mind which we are attempting to discover.

To get a deeper understanding of the nature of mind itself, we can quote the authority of enlightened masters of the lineage as a guide. The third Karmapa, Rangjung Dorje (Rang.byung.rDo rje), wrote a prayer of aspiration for the realization of Mahamudra in which he said, "It is not existent because even the Buddha could not see it, but it is not nonexistent because it is the basis or origin of all samsara and nirvana." It does not constitute a contradiction to say that mind neither exists nor does not exist; it is simultaneously existent and nonexistent.

Let us consider the first part of the statement that the mind does not exist. We take into account that the mind is intangible. One cannot describe it or find it. There is no fixed characteristic that we normally ascribe to things which we can ascribe to mind. Consciousness does not manifest with any particular color, shape, size, form or location. None of these qualities has anything to do with the nature of mind, so we can say that the mind is essentially empty of these limiting characteristics.

Even the fully enlightened Buddha Shakyamuni could not find any thing that is mind, because the mind does not have identifying characteristics. This is what Rangjung Dorje meant when he said, "It does not exist because even the Buddha could not see it."

So, then, is mind nonexistent? No, not in the sense that there is nothing happening. That which experiences confusion, suffering, frustration and all the complexity of samsaric existence is mind itself. This is the origin of all unenlightened experience; it is within the mind that all unenlightened experience happens.

On the other hand, if the individual attains enlightenment, it is mind which is the origin of the enlightened experience, giving expression to the transcending awareness of the various kayas.

This is what Rangjung Dorje meant when he said, "One cannot say that it does not exist, because it is the basis for all samsara and nirvana." Whether we are talking about an enlightened state of being or an unenlightened one, we are speaking about the state of experience that arises from mind and is experienced by the mind. What remains if mind neither exists nor does not exist? According to Rangjung Dorje, this is not a contradiction, but a state of simultaneity. Mind exhibits, at one and the same time, qualities of nonexistence and qualities of existence. To state naively that mind exists is to fall into one error; to deny the existence of anything at all is to fall into another error. This gave rise to the concept of what is called the Middle Way or Madhyamika. Finding a balance between these two beliefs, where there is simultaneous truth to both, is the correct view, according to the Buddha's description of the nature of mind.

When we hear a guru make the statement, "Mind does not exist; mind does not *not* exist; but it is at the same time existent and nonexistent, and this is the middle view," we may say, "Fine, I can accept that," but that is not enough. It is an idea that may appeal to us, a concept with which we are comfortable, but that kind of understanding lacks any real spirit or depth. It is like a patch you put on your clothes to hide a hole. One day the patch will fall off. Intellectual knowledge is rather patchy in that way. It will suffice for the present but it is not ultimately beneficial.

This is not to say that intellectual knowledge is unimportant. It is crucial because it is that which gives us the ability to begin to develop personal experience of what is being discussed. However, mere understanding on a superficial or intellectual level should not be mistaken for the direct experience. We can only arrive at that through meditation and the continued analysis of our own experience. The value of intellectual knowledge is that it is a springboard to deeper, more intuitive experience.

First, then, we say that mind is essentially empty, that it is not describable as some thing. Other than using the label *mind*, there is no thing that could be further described in terms of form, shape, size, color or any distinguishing characteristic.

Beyond this essential emptiness, we can make the statement that mind is like space. Just as space is all-pervasive, so is consciousness. The mind has no problem conceiving of any particular place or experience. While we have attempted to describe the indescribable by saying that mind is essentially empty, that is not the complete picture. We are speaking of something that is like space, but is not space; because if it were space, it would not be mind, it would be space. We are speaking of something that is obviously qualitatively different from simple space. We need to remember that when we are using these terms, we are attempting to describe something that is indescribable. However, that does not mean that it cannot be directly experienced. The person who is mute is still able to experience the sweetness of sugar without being able to describe it to anyone else. Just as the mute person has trouble describing the taste of sugar, we have trouble describing the nature of mind, but we try our best. We search for examples and metaphors that will give us some idea of what is being experienced.

Another aspect of the nature of mind is its luminosity. Normally we think of this term in a visual sense. We think of a luminous body like the sun or the moon which shines and gives off light. However, this is merely a metaphor to give us some idea of what is being hinted at. To say that the mind is luminous in nature is analogous to saying that space is illuminated. For example, we can have empty space and there might be no illumination; then the space would be obscured. There is space, but no ability to see clearly; there is no direct experience possible in complete darkness. Just as there is clear vision in illuminated space, so in the same way, while mind is essentially empty, it exhibits the potential to know, which is its luminosity. This is not a visual experience per se, but the ability of mind to know, perceive and experience.

In our continuing attempt to describe the nature of mind, to describe the indescribable, we next speak of the unimpeded or unobstructed dynamic nature of mind. It will be useful to divide this element of unimpededness into a subtle and a gross aspect. The most subtle or fundamental level of the unimpeded quality is an awareness of the emptiness and luminosity of the mind. The mind is essentially empty and has this illuminating potential to know and experience.

The coarse or gross aspect of the unimpeded dynamic manifestation of mind is conscious experience, which does not depart from emptiness and luminosity, but is the experience of, for example, seeing and recognizing form as form, hearing and recognizing sound as sound, and so forth. This is the ability of mind to experience the phenomenal world, to make distinctions, to make value judgments based upon that discrimination.

We may utilize a metaphor here. The emptiness of mind is the ocean; the luminosity of mind is the sunlit ocean; and the unimpeded dynamic quality of mind is the waves of the sunlit ocean. When we take the waves of the sunlit ocean as an event or situation, it is not as though we are trying to separate ocean from waves from sunlight; they are three aspects of a single experience. The unity of these three aspects forms the seed or potential for enlightenment. They are the pure nature of mind; the impurity of obscurations, ignorance and confusion overlays what is inherently the nature of mind itself.

There has always been the pure nature of mind and there has always been fundamental ignorance in the mind. The essential empty nature of mind has never been recognized for what it is; the luminous nature of mind has never been experienced for what it is; and the unimpeded or dynamic manifestation of mind, this consciousness, this awareness, has never been directly experienced for what it is. Because this level of ignorance is so subtle and so fundamental, and because it is co-existent with mind itself, it has been valid as long as mind itself has been valid. We speak of it as co-emergent ignorance.

Just as there are subtle and gross aspects to the dynamic awareness of mind that we noted earlier, there are subtler and coarser aspects to the ignorance of mind. We have already spoken of the fundamental level of co-emergent ignorance, the lack of direct experience of the empty, clear and unimpeded nature of mind itself, and this is the subtle aspect of co-emergent ignorance.

There is a second level of ignorance that we might distinguish which is termed labelling ignorance; it is a more conventional or relative ignorance. Not only do we lack direct experience of the essential emptiness of mind, for example, but we substitute the self or ego for that experience. The individual mind as something ultimately real is a distortion that has taken place, due to a lack of direct experience, and this is an example of labelling or relative ignorance. Likewise, due to a lack of direct experience of the clarity and luminosity of mind, there is a projection of something other than the mind, an object other than the subject. This is again a relative level of ignorance. Rather than being a simple lack of direct experience, there has been a distortion into some *thing*.

So the second level of obscuration in the mind is the aspect of ignorance which begins to label things as I and other. Lacking direct experience, the distortion takes place on a coarser level of dualistic fixation between subject and object.

Once we have this dualistic framework, of course, emotionality develops and action takes place. Karmic tendencies are reinforced by actions based on the emotional confusion which springs from dualistic clinging. All of it is based upon the fundamental ignorance which is the lack of direct experience of the nature of the mind itself.

The nature of mind is like empty space, like the sky, which at present is filled with clouds and fog and mist and periodically has all kinds of activity such as hailstorms, snowstorms, rainstorms and thunder and lightning. This activity does not change the fact that the empty space is still present, the sky is still there. However, it is temporarily obscured by all these activities. The reason the Buddha presented his teachings, which encourage basic moral choices between virtuous and nonvirtuous actions and encourage the practice of meditation, is to eliminate the obscuring and confusing aspects of our experience. This permits the inherently pure nature of mind to become more obvious and be discovered, just as the sun becomes more obvious as the clouds begin to dissipate.

As the most effective means to bring about that transformation rapidly and directly, the Mahamudra approach has no equal. It gives us the most powerful methods to turn the balance, to eliminate obscurations and allow that manifestation to take place. Our present situation as unenlightened beings is due to the victory of ignorance over intrinsic awareness; Mahamudra speeds the victory of awareness over ignorance.

When we are concerned with foundation Mahamudra, then, we first and foremost need to be exposed to ideas. This should take place in the presence of a teacher who holds the transmission and can accurately introduce us to the concepts which are the theoretical underpinnings of the Mahamudra approach. After we receive the teachings and understand what is being said, we take them home with us and begin to apply them to our own experience. We say to ourselves, "Well, mind is empty, clear and unimpeded. What do I experience when I experience mind? Does it exist; does it not exist?" We check with our own experience. That is very beneficial for developing a kind of mental construct from which we can work, though it is not the ultimate experience. Conceptual understanding is only a springboard, because the theme of Mahamudra is spontaneity and uncontrivedness, and it is still a very contrived situation to *think* of the mind as being empty. To directly experience the nature of mind itself requires meditation.

So on this foundation level of Mahamudra, the analytical approach is followed by, and interwoven with, the more intuitive approach of relaxing the mind in its own natural state. The particular skill required is that it must be a state of total relaxation which is not distracted or dull. It is not an objective experience of looking for the mind or looking at the mind. On the other hand, it is not a blind process; we are not unaware. There is seeing without looking; there is dwelling in the experience without looking at the experience. This is the keynote of the intuitive approach.

While the mind is poised in the state of bare awareness, there is no directing the mind. One is not looking within for anything; one is not looking without for anything. One is simply letting the mind rest in its own natural state. The empty, clear and unimpeded nature of mind can be experienced if we can rest in an uncontrived state of bare awareness without distraction and without the spark of awareness being lost. The pure nature of mind calls to mind an image such as the sun or the moon, a luminous body. The unimpeded nature of mind permits the act of thinking of this form in the first place, and we can rest in the bare perception of that form without any further elaboration; we dwell in the bare awareness of that form.

Thus one's approach in developing the foundation aspect of Mahamudra is, at times, an analytical or conceptual approach of examining the mind from the point of view of trying to locate it, describe it or define it, and at other times an intuitive approach of dwelling in the experience of total relaxation of mind, an uncontrived state of bare awareness which allows the experience of the nature of mind to arise.

The third Karmapa wrote a prayer in which he said that confidence comes of clearly establishing the parameters of practice by defining the nature of mind precisely. Then the confidence of actually experiencing and appreciating it on an intuitive level completes the foundation. The prayer describes meditation as remaining true to that experience by refining through continual attention to and absorption in that experience. Path Mahamudra is the refining of and attending to the basic experience of the nature of mind. When we remain true to this experience of the nature of mind and refine it, then at a certain point, an automatic quality arises; the experience happens without one generating it or discovering it. The mind is subject to very little distraction at all. When this occurs, one has entered into the level of path Mahamudra which is termed *one-pointedness* or focus on a single thing. In this case, the focus is on a single aspect of experience, the experience of mind nature. Traditionally there are three degrees of this one-pointed experience: a lesser degree of intensity, an intermediate one, and a very intense degree.

As meditation continues, the next clearly definable stage is a certain spontaneity, where the experience is no longer the result of any particular effort; to think of meditation is to have the experience. One begins to discover the incredible simplicity of the nature of mind, absolutely free from any complication and this, in fact, is the name given to the second phase of experience, *simplicity*, the freedom from complication. Traditionally this phase also has three degrees of intensity; a lesser degree, an intermediate degree, and a very intense degree.

In the beginning, one is meditating for short and frequent periods of time rather than attempting long periods of forcing the mind. But as experience accumulates and simplicity arises, one's meditation naturally begins to be of longer and longer duration. Soon the phase termed *one flavor* arises, which is the experience of the essential quality of all aspects of phenomenal experience. Soon, seeing form, hearing sounds, smelling smells, tasting tastes, feeling textures, thinking thoughts, formless states of awareness and form states of awareness all have the same flavor. One perceives the underlying essential nature of these experiences, rather than being concerned with the superficial content. This is the third phase of the experience of path Mahamudra, the unique flavor of all aspects of one's experience, and again, it has different degrees of intensity forming a spectrum of experience, rather than clearly defined steps.

The spontaneity of the experience will take over completely so that there seems no need to meditate at all. The experience arises without there being any particular thought of meditating. This is a glimpse which intensifies further to become the actual experience of the nature of mind without there being any thought of meditation. The most intense degree of this stage is that meditation and being become one. At that point there is no longer any distinction between meditating and not meditating because one is always meditating. The full experience of this is the most intense degree of the fourth phase of path Mahamudra which is termed *beyond meditation*. The sustained experience of this phase is the result of all one's efforts, Mahamudra. It is the quintessential experience, the pinnacle experience in terms of the attainment of enlightenment and realization.

It is important to identify the context of the Mahamudra experience. Tradition assures us that any approach, other than one's own efforts at purifying and developing oneself and the blessing that one receives from an authentic and qualified guru, is stupid. Of course, at a certain point, the practice becomes spontaneous and the efforts to purify oneself and to develop devotion to receive blessings from one's guru become second nature. However, this does not become spontaneous until the intense level of the simplicity experience, the second phase of Mahamudra practice, when the practice of meditation becomes one's purification, one's development and the receipt of blessing from one's guru. The fundamental identity of the guru's mind and one's own mind begins to be directly perceptible; one's deepening awareness assures further development of merit and the further purification of obscurations and negativity; there is no necessity to formally supplicate one's guru, meditate upon one's guru or generate devotion in order to receive blessing, because the meditation practice carries one along.

Up to that point, however, the efforts that we make to purify ourselves, to develop our devotion and open ourselves to the guru's blessing are absolutely crucial. Only present exertions will convey us to the time when they are no longer necessary; the practice of meditation becomes the process of purification, the process of development and the process of receiving blessing.

CHAPTER FOURTEEN

CONCLUDING REMARKS

There are some final remarks I would like to make as these teachings come to a close. I give this advice to my students from the perspective of being someone who is reasonably old now and originally came from far off in the hills of eastern Tibet. Having travelled the world, East and West, I have been impressed by the energy and effort that one sees people in all countries putting into the progress and development of their country. They work to consolidate some kind of material progress, security and prosperity for themselves and their country.

Nowhere does one find this more in evidence than in a country like the United States. It is a very large and prosperous country, with a very high standard of living and a very high degree of personal freedom when compared to other situations. There is far more freedom in America than elsewhere to go where one wants, to do what one wants, to practice the religion that one wants, and to work as one wishes. In America, one is free to pursue the bettering of oneself, the consolidation of one's business, one's security and prosperity and so forth.

On the other hand, there is the problem of taxes, but I do not see any real evil being committed on this level, because it seems to be only fair that if people earn money, the government should take some of it for social services and things which benefit the people as a whole. This is like something arising from the ocean and dissolving back into the ocean; it arises from the people and then dissolves back into the people and tends to even out on a large scale. It is difficult to find another country where as much attention is paid to the old people, children, orphans, sick people and needy people, at least on a relative level. There is a kind of benevolence in this society which needs to be brought to everyone's attention. There is a kind of parental role in government and a public feeling in this country which is concerned with people in less fortunate circumstances.

Also, where else could one find so much available, so much that could answer anyone's wishes. If one wants the smallest article of clothing, one can get it in white, red, black, yellow and blue. One can get any kind of clothing one wants; one can even go without clothing if one wants. In general as I have experienced the way things are run in this country, there is a great deal to be said for it and far less to be said against it. The basic structure of this society and the way it is governed offer much to the people in it, and this is something people need to be aware of, because it is very easy to find fault and complain.

In this particular time, of course, the problems which are facing the world, particularly that of nuclear warfare, and the danger of very widespread destruction, are ever-present. There is an understandable wave of sentiment throughout the world now to disarm the world completely; this is, of course, a goal to which we always need to aspire, because the basic function of weaponry is to hurt, harm, or injure. As long as this weaponry exists, then the danger exists that it will be used. So an ideal which is very worthy is the hope that efforts can be made to eliminate this threat from the world, so that humans will not have to suffer the consequences. As I see it, this can be viewed in at least two ways. The first is the ideal, that we would all hope for, that it would be possible at some point in the future to bring peace to the world. Weaponry would be a thing of the past and the world would not need that particular way of relating in order to survive.

However, from the realistic point of view, one must not be too over-zealous in making oneself vulnerable. If one country such as America abandons its weapons when other countries do not, there remains the risk of being invaded and losing the benefits that do exist in this culture, which would be a great loss. This topic is one which must be viewed from a global and a realistic perspective. It is a very difficult thing for me to make any definitive choice.

The reason why there exist so many religions in the world, so many spiritual traditions, is because the enlightened compassion of Buddhas and Bodhisattvas manifests in different ways in different circumstances to meet different needs. In some cases greater needs will be met; in some cases lesser or intermediate needs will be met. Nevertheless, there is benefit to be found in all these situations. The ability of these spiritual traditions to continue to develop and flourish in the world is a very important factor in the future happiness of humanity. Thus, it always gives me pleasure to come to a country such as America where there is this personal freedom for one to practice the religion of one's choice and for religions to establish themselves, even though they may be very new to this country. The benefits of living in this country are numerous, and my general advice to you is to be aware of these benefits and take advantage of them.

More specifically, my journeys began in 1971, and I have visited North America four times. A number of centers and groups started up as a result of my coming and teaching in North America. I was particularly concerned with the problem of lamas or teachers to stay in these centers, because I felt this was one very crucial factor in insuring the stability and development of a center: that it have a resident teacher. I went to His Holiness the Sixteenth Gyalwa Karmapa and asked him personally to look into this, to do what he could to send lamas who are qualified to be resident teachers in these centers. After I made this request, he replied to me that it was basically my function to supply the lamas. He would supply the passes and visas that they needed to assure them passage to the West but since I had founded the centers, it was appropriate for me to supply the teachers.

At that point, the pool of potential lamas that we were drawing upon were Tibetans, Bhutanese and Sikkimese. These were the people who had received the training in the Kagyu teachings that would qualify them to act as teachers in Kagyu centers. However, we ran into a problem, because most of them were quite aware of the fact that in leaving India, Sikkim, Bhutan or Nepal and going to the West, they were travelling an immense distance; they were severing their roots and ties with the culture they had grown up in, and they were going to a completely foreign culture. People did not speak the same language, wear the same clothes, or eat the same food. The entire situation was different and they would be going there alone, which did not strike them as a particularly entertaining prospect.

His Holiness would instruct these lamas, "You know I want you to go to the West. We are trying to set up centers in the West." But what we originally found was that people balked at this, though it was done in a rather roundabout way, because they couldn't simply go to someone like His Holiness and say no. One does not do that with someone like His Holiness. He tends not to listen when one says no, so when he would say, "You go to the West," they would say, "Well, you know, my poor old father is just about on his deathbed," or, "My mother really needs me to take care of her," or "You know I have this sickness and the doctor says I can't travel."

My particular advantage is that I am not someone great like His Holiness, so that if I tell someone to do something, they can argue with me. They can always say, "Well, okay, but isn't it going to be difficult?" They know that when I send them somewhere, if things turn out to be difficult, they can write and tell me about it. They can let me know, "Look, things are really hard here," and there is the chance that I will help them by sending a replacement or doing whatever I can. They do not feel so locked into the situation if I tell them to go to the West.

The first lama that I established in the West was Lama Tsengyur Rinpoche at Vancouver, British Columbia in 1971. Following that, there was a second wave of lamas to the West, which included Lama Lodö of San Francisco, and a third wave which included Lama Karma Dorje of Santa Fe. In the future there will be more lamas coming to stay in cities in the West.

The result of founding centers and sending teachers has been a significant growth and spread of the teachings in the West. Slowly but surely the centers are getting themselves on a firm basis and actually being able to branch out. The center in San Francisco has land which is providing the opportunity for a three-year, three-month retreat center to be built in the future. Projects like this are going on all over the world and that is cause for celebration.

On a purely mundane level, we are all aware of the fact that the more power and influence and wealth one has, the more problems and complications there are in one's life. There is an analogy to this on the spiritual level, because the more profound one's practice, the more profound are the obstacles one is likely to encounter. As much effort as one makes in developing one's positive qualities, one is quite likely to find that there are equal responses, either from inner negativity and obscuration in one's own character or negative forces in the world around one, and each of these cause obstructions. This seems to be something of an equation; the deeper the practice, the deeper the obstacles.

One of the most serious obstacles from the point of view of one's practice of dharma, is disharmony the falling out with one's spiritual teachers, one's center of dharma, one's vajra brothers and sisters; in so doing one is really cutting oneself off from the benefit that one has personally received from these sources. Of course we all know the way of the world is one of friction and conflict. It seems to be part of so-called human nature that friction can increase to the point that a situation becomes unworkable. This is a very grave thing if it happens on the spiritual level. Harmony between teachers and students, and between students and students who are brothers and sisters in the teaching, is very important; the concept of samaya, the bond or commitment one has to another, due to the connections one has through teachings and practice, is a very crucial element in one's spiritual development. To cause serious ruptures of samaya is something which will cause much unhappiness and suffering in this life, and also turn the mind toward lower states of existence contrary to the spiritual path.

The resident teachers at centers in the West may function as lamas by having students who have faith in them and have accepted them as gurus; or they may function as teachers in the ordinary sense of the word. Some people may not have faith in them as gurus or are not prepared to approach them on that level, but will approach them as instructors in the dharma, people qualified through their own experience and understanding of the teachings to talk about and explain the teachings. One could even think of them as a kind of translator or conduit for information that has been transmitted from the Kagyu lineage. Regardless of the particular way in which one relates to the resident teacher of the center, the connection remains a very positive and important one.

Faith and confidence is an interesting phenomenon because the benefits are so personal. If one has faith in a very worthy principle or person, one can receive tremendous blessing. The Tibetans tell a story to illustrate this which concerns an individual named Ben who came from an area known as Köngpo in southeastern Tibet. He was called Köngpo Ben and he was an extremely simple fellow who was gullible but had a great deal of faith.

Ben had heard much about the Jowo Rinpoche or Precious Lord in Lhasa, which is a very beautiful statue of the Buddha Shakyamuni as a young prince. This is one of the most holy and important images in the whole of Tibet and it rests in a cathedral known as the Jokhang, the Lord's House. Ben was not quite sure if it was a god or a man or what, but he was determined to go see for himself what the Precious Lord was all about. So he put on his boots and got his knapsack and his stick and went walking through southeastern Tibet for weeks and weeks to get to Lhasa, the capital in central Tibet.

When he arrived there, he asked his way, and found himself in the Jokhang. There was the beautiful smiling statue of the Buddha and he walked up to it and said, "Oh, I'm very glad to be here; I've heard a lot about you and I'm very glad to meet you." He stood smiling and nodding to the statue and the statue smiled back benignly.

Since he had walked such a long way, Ben was quite hungry and thirsty. He looked around and saw a table in front of the image on which people had put all kinds of butter lamps and special cakes which are made as offerings for the shrine. Ben thought to himself, "Hmm, some kind person has put these out for the Precious Lord and his visitors to eat." He took one of the cakes and dipped it into one of the butter lamps and ate it while looking up at the figure which was still smiling benignly at him. He thought to himself, "What a nice lama that is."

When he was no longer hungry and thirsty, he said, "I wonder if you could watch my things for me; I'm just going to do a quick circumambulation around you just as a sign of respect and then I'll be back." The statue replied, "Yes," so he took off his muddy old boots and his knapsack and stick and put them down in front of the image and off he went to do his circumambulation.

While he was circumambulating this rather large building, the custodian of the shrine came in and saw to his horror that somebody had been disturbing the offerings and leaving their dirty boots in front of the statue. Outraged, the custodian was throwing them out the door of the cathedral when he heard the statue say, "Köngpo Ben left those and told me to watch after them. Leave them here."

Köngpo Ben had a very basic faith. He spent many days in Lhasa visiting the Precious Lord and having audience with him. When he was ready to return to his home country, he said, "Why don't you visit me during the harvest? I've got a field of barley and we can make some good barley flour and brew up some barley beer. I have a friend who can slaughter a pig and we'll have a real feast going. I'll be happy to really host you in style." The statue said he would come, so Ben started his long journey.

When Köngpo Ben finally returned home, his wife greeted him and asked him if he had accomplished his goal. He said, "Oh yes, I met the Precious Lord, and he's a very fine lama. I've invited him to come in the ninth month, so we'll have to prepare then for this very honored guest."

When the ninth month came, he said to his wife, "Whenever you go outside, look for signs that someone special is coming." One day when she went to the river for water, the river was glowing as if the sun were shining up from under the water, and she thought, "That's it!" She went running back to her husband and said, "I think he's here. I went down to the river and there's this light in it that I've never seen before." Her husband told her to put on the tea water and went running down to the river.

When he got there, he could see the form of the Precious Lord in the river. He thought the Lord was drowning so he dove in the water and came up with the form of the Precious Lord, and they had a nice chat. Then Ben carried the Precious Lord along the road and when they came to a certain bend in the road where there was a large rock face, the Precious Lord said to him, "I won't be visiting you," and he dissolved into the rock face. To this day in southeastern Tibet, there are two special places to visit. One is the rock face in which there is a form of the Buddha, and the other is a form of the Buddha which can be seen in a certain river. These are known as the Water Lord and the Rock Lord and are famous sites of pilgrimage.

Köngpo Ben's was a situation where blessings and benefits arose from faith in something very exalted and noble. This does not preclude the possibility of someone receiving the same kind of benefit even if the object of faith is quite ordinary; it is the quality of faith that counts. The Tibetans tell another story to illustrate faith in something ordinary.

There was an old woman in Lhasa whose son was a trader. Once a year he went to India to do business. His mother was a very devout Buddhist. She said to her son on numerous occasions, as he was setting off on his trips, "You know, you're going to the land of India, which is the most holy country on earth as far as Buddhists are concerned, because the Lord Buddha appeared there and first presented the teachings of Buddhadharma in that country. Do your old mother a favor and bring back some relic or some holy article or object from India that I can use as an object of worship on my shrine. I'll place it on my shrine and do prostrations to it, pray to it, make offerings to it as a way to develop my faith and merit."

Every time the son would say, "Yes, mother," but he would become so involved in his business that he would completely forget about it, because to him it was a very trivial thing. When he would return, his mother would ask, "Well, did you bring me my relic?" And he would tell her he'd forgotten. This was repeated many times.

As she got older, the woman became a little desperate and she finally said to her son, "This may be the last journey you will make in my lifetime. This is your last chance to bring me a holy relic from India. If you fail, this old mother of yours is going to kill herself in your presence." Realizing she was serious, he tried his best to remember, but again he became involved in travelling, trading, and making profits.

On his return journey, he sat by the side of the road to brew up a cup of tea. Suddenly, he remembered his promise to his mother and in his desperation, saw the bones of a dog that had died by the side of the road. He had an inspiration and broke off one of the teeth from the jawbone of the dog, wrapped it up in very fine silk of different colors, and carried it home.

When his mother said, "Did you remember?" he said, "I remembered." He unwrapped his gift and said, "This is the Buddha's tooth. I brought this back from India just for you, Mother, because you wanted something very holy. It is a very, very blessed and holy object." His mother was overjoyed. She took it and put it on the crown of her head and then put it up on her shrine. She would spend the whole day doing prostrations to it, making offerings to it and praying to the Buddha in the presence of what she felt was the tooth of the Buddha. The remarkable thing was that relics started to emerge from this dog's tooth. Not only did these benefit a large number of people, but the old woman was enveloped in a rainbow of light as she died and a shower of blossoms rained down from the sky as an indication that she had definitely made a significant step forward on the path to liberation.

So, even in situations where the object of one's faith seems to be quite ordinary, one should never exclude the possibility that one's faith and confidence in that situation will open one to a great deal of blessing and benefit. This in fact was the basis for the proverb in Tibet that says, "Even a dog's tooth can give off relics."

In sending resident teachers to centers, I considered the fact that these people have been involved in the practice and study of dharma from a very early age, that they have spent their lives trying to practice and to understand as much as they can, and that they have all done the three-year, three-month retreat program of training in meditation and study which qualifies them as a teacher. When I see the needs of centers, I feel that to send such an individual is beneficial. I only send someone who I feel is going to be helpful for the situation. It seems to me that the people I send do their best, out of affection and compassion for the people at that center, to direct and guide the development of the center as best they can. Perhaps the source of one's faith is an excellent one, such as the story about the old man and the statue; on the other hand, perhaps we are in a very ordinary situation, but let us not forget that dog's teeth can bring out relics for those of us who have faith.

This should not be interpreted as saying, "You must have faith in such and such a situation." Even someone like His Holiness the Dalai Lama or His Holiness the Gyalwa Karmapa would not say that. One should discover one's own faith. It remains an entirely personal decision. The only thing a spiritual teacher can say is, "It is very good to have faith." Faith is a very positive and beneficial quality to have in a spiritual context. At the very least, one can regard a lama as someone like a parent or teacher in school who is doing their best to help in the situation. It is important when there is a lama in the center for there to be harmonious relationships. The members should respect the lama as they would their parents or their teachers. It is also necessary for the lama to have an affectionate and compassionate view toward the students and members of the center and the same concern and commitment as a parent.

When there is harmony, then things can only develop for the good. In addition, there is the concept of samaya, the commitment that one receives when one begins Vajrayana or tantric practice. When one is associated with a center, with other people, and a teacher, and when one has received the same teachings and empowerments and transmissions, one shares a very strong bond with those individuals as one's vajra brothers and sisters. Harmony is especially important on this level, because it is that which contributes to the extreme rapidity of the tantric path. To deliberately spurn that bond is correspondingly very negative. So, harmony becomes important not only on a general social level of benevolence and good will, but also on a level of samaya. One has taken on oneself a commitment that must be respected.

In a center, the lama is the head and the students and members of the center are the body. One cannot live and work without the other. There is a sense of a collective experience as they travel together to the highest heights; if the samaya is broken, they will all go down together. If lamas and students can work together in harmony, then I see nothing but positive development in the future.

What, you may ask, is the purpose of all the empowerments, teachings and transmissions that one receives? They function to further one on the path to liberation. This should not imply that there is no effort on one's own part. One's own physical, mental and verbal involvement in virtuous and positive action and spiritual practice is a very significant factor in receiving the benefits of the teachings and transmissions that one has received.

As a way to develop one's practice of the dharma, the importance of the fundamentals cannot be overemphasized. The most fundamental aspect of one's practice of the dharma is the taking of refuge. We have already discussed the sources of refuge: the Three Jewels of Buddha, Dharma, and Sangha; and the Three Roots of the Vajrayana practice, guru, meditational divinities and dharma protectors. As for someone practicing the dharma, one needs to renew this sense of taking refuge each and every day, if not more frequently. At least when one first awakens, one can renew the commitment through the recitation of taking refuge. It is important to give something from the heart during this recitation.

Also, the element of bodhicitta, the enlightening element of altruistic compassion and concern for others in one's spiritual practice, cannot be overemphasized. Every morning when one has renewed one's commitment through taking refuge, it is important to renew the samaya of bodhicitta as well. One may recite, "This day, whatever I take part in, physically, verbally or mentally, may this be for the benefit of all beings. I aspire to help all beings in all situations as much as possible." Whether it is in this simple context or in a formal spiritual practice during the day, if one has those two as a basis to work from, then one will find one's mind coming more and more into the dharma, and the Dharma will become more and more a path for one. In a certain sense, this arises from the fact that one is emphasizing the foundations and the practice develops from that.

The Tara meditation is an excellent morning practice and is offered at many centers. The particular function of the Bodhisattva Tara is to remove fear and obstacles. The efficacy of the practice relates to all kinds of threats or fears in the external environment, which can prove to be serious obstacles for one's well-being and also for one's spiritual practice.

The Mahakala ritual is often offered at centers in the evening. This protective influence shelters one's practice against obstacles, whether they arise from within oneself, one's own negativity, or from the external situation. The Six-armed Mahakala practice carries particular protection and benefit which is realized in the Bardo or after-death state.

Chenrezig, the bodhisattva of compassion, is one of the single most basic and powerful forms upon which to meditate; it is also an extremely simple practice which is imbued with very profound implications in terms of one's spiritual development. Because of the great benefit of the practice, and the relative ease with which one can learn to put it into practice, I have felt that it is a very worthy meditation for centers to use as their main focus.

Whether one approaches resident lamas as gurus, as teachers, as translators or channels of information, they exist for the purpose of transmitting that information on one level or another to the people who are interested in using those techniques.

To conclude these teachings, it is important to dedicate the merit and virtue. We are inspired to follow the examples of the Buddhas, Bodhisattvas and spiritual teachers in our attempt to share the benefits of spiritual practice for the good of all. The particular benefits that we derive from spiritual practice depend upon our own efforts and on our own perceptions of spiritual practice. Dedicating our efforts to others encourages us to develop positive qualities conducive to spiritual development and to eliminate negative, harmful tendencies and actions in our way of life. In the last analysis, it all comes down to this: our personal efforts to make the distinctions between virtue and nonvirtue and to make the appropriate choices based on those distinctions.

QUESTIONS OF GENERAL INTEREST

What are the karmic implications if terminally ill people voluntarily take themselves off of life support? If they are in a coma, what are the karmic consequences of their families removing them from life support, allowing them to die? What can someone who is working with the terminally ill do to prepare them for death?

It is very difficult to say something simple about such a complex situation. Perhaps the most basic observation to make is that from the point of view of the person who is working with the terminally ill patient, the crucial difference would seem to be whether that person's basic motivation is one of compassion and concern for the patient in trying to alleviate suffering and preferably, cure the disease. If that is the basic motivating factor, then it is very doubtful that the healer or therapist will do anything wrong karmically. We may not be able to save the patient's life. We may not be able to relieve the person's suffering. But we are trying our best, motivated in the purest way possible. Whatever we do, even if it is not ultimately successful, can never be thought of as karmically damaging or karmically negative.

If we are negligent, if we deliberately abuse the patient's health out of carelessness or lack of concern, then of course, that is a different matter. We are not motivated by basic concern, nor do we have the proper commitment to the patient's well-being, and there are different karmic consequences.

The person who decides that they have had enough suffering and wishes to be allowed to die is in a situation that we cannot call virtuous or nonvirtuous. We certainly cannot blame someone for making that decision. It is not a karmically negative act. It is simply the wish to avoid suffering, which is a fundamental wish of all living beings. On the other hand, it is not a particularly virtuous act, either. It is a karmically neutral act to decide in that situation not to allow one's disease to run its course and kill one. Rather than being a wish to end one's life, it's a wish to end suffering. Therefore, it is a karmically neutral act.

When a healer is instructed by a patient to remove life support systems, that puts the healer in a difficult position, because the instincts of the healer may be telling them, "If this person stayed on the life support system they would remain alive. If I take them off, they will die." The karmic consequences depend upon the healer's intent, because the healer will be depriving someone of the means to stay alive, regardless of the fact that it was that person that told us to do it. If the basic motivation of the healer has always been to help and benefit that person and relieve their suffering, then, from that state of mind, it seems as though nothing karmically negative can develop.

Do the skandhas, the psychophysical aggregates of an individual's character, arise as aspects of ignorance? How can we use them as concepts? Also, can we utilize the Six Perfections of the Mahayana as antidotes to particular mental poisons or emotional complexes?

We can think of the skandhas, the aggregates of our psychophysical character, as manifestations or aspects of ignorance, but then, what isn't an aspect of ignorance from the point of view of an unenlightened being? The entirety of our experience, the universe that we experience, is, on one level or another, a manifestation of our ignorance. So, from that point of view, it is not a particularly remarkable statement to say that the skandhas are aspects of ignorance. In fact, they are an attempt to describe the totality of a given being's mental and physical experience.

The skandhas are the five aggregates of form, sensation, perception, volition or formation, and consciousness. The first is fairly easy to understand. It refers to the phenomenal world and the physical body, the form aspect of our experience, from the physical body which is compounded of atoms and molecules; to the external world with its various objects and phenomena which may be tangible and composed of atomic matter, or its intangible experiences such as sound.

The second skandha, that of sensation, is partly physical and partly mental. There are already physical sensations due to the fact that there is the form skandha, involving the physical body as one of its components. Based upon the physical body, we have sensations of heat and cold and pain and pleasure and so forth. There are also purely mental sensations of suffering and wellbeing, of happiness and unhappiness and so forth, and so this skandha has both physical elements and purely mental elements.

Perception, volition, and consciousness are a little more subtle and the best way to think of these three is not as three separate things but as different points on a continuum that runs from pre-conscious perception to conscious experience. The best example we might think of is that of the surface of the ocean when a wave begins to form. First there is a swelling of the water in one direction or another, a shift due to the motion of the wind or tide. This swelling is like perception. Once there is an initial perception of heat or cold or whatever, this begins to stir the mind toward actual conscious experience.

The next stage is like the wave actually beginning to form, the water moving up into a kind of peak. This is analagous to volition, which is not yet conscious experience but is, for example, in seeing a form, the clear presentation of that form to the mind's eye through the organ of sight. The mind becomes perfectly aware of the form as a form before recognizing it as a particular form with particular characteristics.

In the fifth skandha, that of actual conscious experience, the mind perceives that each form is a particular kind of form which is good or bad or neutral. There is an evaluation of experience at that point which is conscious mental activity, and that is like the wave actually cresting, as a fully defined wave. Thus this scheme of the five skandhas is an attempt to describe the totality of our experience, physical and mental.

In regard to the Six Perfections of the Mahayana path, generosity, morality, patience, exertion, meditative stability and wisdom, these are specific techniques or attitudes that are particularly beneficial and effective for our spiritual development. We could arrange it neatly so that each one of these paramitas or perfections is related to a particular emotion. For example, we could say that, of the six fundamental emotions which the texts make reference to, one is avarice or greed. Generosity is the antidote to avarice or greed; we share instead of take. We could arrange it that way, but each one of the paramitas is actually an effective antidote for any negative emotion.

Rinpoche, my father has become senile. I am wondering how to share the Dharma with him before he dies.

We are dealing with a number of limitations, because, for example, it is doubtful that your father was someone who was particularly inclined toward Buddhism even when he had all of his mental faculties. To approach him on a formal level of explaining the teachings is not only something which is severely limited due to his declining awareness and intelligence, but is also something to which he has not been predisposed. In this situation, the benefit that the teachings could give him would be perhaps in the form of your recitation of mantras or the names of Buddhas in his presence. You will be planting seeds. Your own aspirations and altruistic concern for him in this situation are very important. In offering this service to your father in his unhappy circumstances, you must go about it with the best of intentions, out of a true concern for his welfare and happiness. That is a very important factor in your relationship to him in these times.

The most important thing is that you have a very strong connection to him as his daughter. The karmic connection between parents and children is very strong. Much benefit can be worked on subtle levels because of that bond, if our approach to our parents is marked by compassion and concern and our involvement in spiritual practice is not only for our own sake, but for the benefit of other beings as well, particularly, in this case, our parents.

How do you feel about the threat of nuclear war and the spread of Buddhism in North America, as two parts of our present experience?

The spread of Buddhism represents one very great source of hope, because the more people who involve themselves in the dharma, or, rather, the more people who are behaving in ways which are in accord with the dharma, the better the entire situation becomes. The Buddha frequently said that the experience of the human race as a whole depends upon the behavior of the human race as a whole. If the vast majority are engaged in unskillful and harmful and evil actions, the general situation degenerates rapidly; if the majority of people become involved in spiritual practice, or at least in activity which is in accordance with spiritual practice, then the general situation improves. It is a collective result of the individual actions of human beings that determines the collective experience of beings in the human realm, for better or for worse.

GLOSSARY

Arhat (Tib: dgra.bcom.pa) *Foe or enemy destroyer.* Designates a level of accomplishment where the enemy, dualistic ego-clinging, has been conquered.

Bardo (Tib: bar.do) Bardo literally refers to any *intemtediate state of existence;* virtually any transition is a bardo. However, in the context of the Buddha's teachings, the Holy Dharma, this term most often refers to the transition which begins when a person dies and continues until that person is reborn.

Bodhicitta (Tib: byang.sems) *Pure enlightenment attitude.* There is both a relative and an absolute bodhicitta. Relative bodhicitta rises from the practitioner's meditation upon and generation of compassion for other sentient beings (see **Bodhisattva**). This leads to glimpses of absolute bodhicitta, the true nature of reality, which is all-pervasive and effortless compassion for all beings. In turn, this inspires more compassion for beings and the intent to deliver them from samsara.

Bodhisattva (Tib: byang.chub.sems.dpa') In general, this term applies to anyone who has taken the vow to relinquish their personal enlightenment in order to work for the benefit of all sentient beings. More specifically, it designates a special class of beings who have not only taken that vow but who also have attained a significant level of realization.

Buddha (Tib: sangs.rgyas) The word has two parts in Tibetan, *sangs* and *rgyas* respectively. The first means clear and unstained by the defilements of attachment, aversion, and ignorance. The second refers to the attainment of all-pervasive wisdom. Normally we think of the word as denoting the historical Buddha, Shakyamuni, but it is just as often used to refer to the principle of enlightenment which all beings possess.

Dakini (Tib: mkha'.'gro.ma) *One who goes in the sky.* There are many different kinds and levels of dakinis. In general, the word refers to certain female meditational deities or yidams. It can also describe female celestial messengers and protectors or female bodhisattvas who are performing actions for the benefit of sentient beings.

Dharmapala See **Dharma Protector**

Dharma Protector (Tib: chos.skyong) *Guardian of the Buddha's Teaching.* This term is most often, but not exclusively, applied to wrathful deities who have taken a vow to protect the Holy Dharma and, in some cases, those who practice it. These protectors may be invoked by an individual practitioner in order to protect his/her practice from either external negative influences or the negative influence of their own mental poisons.

Ganachakra (Tib: tshogs) This is a divine feast offering which traditionally may follow an important event like a meditation or the conclusion of the visit of an important lama. Unlike an ordinary feast, the ganachakra feast is imbued with such symbolism that it can become a meditational practice itself for those who partake. For example, the solid foods (like meat) and liquid foods (like wine) symbolize skillful means and wisdom respectively. Thus, even those who have vows against eating certain of these foods will consume them during a ganachakra.

Guru (Tib: bla.ma) *Master, teacher.* Although in English this word has come to refer to any teacher or monk, technically it refers only to enlightened masters.

Hinayana (Tib: theg.chung) *Lesser Vehicle.* The Hinayana is comprised of the paths of the Shravaka and Pratyekabuddha. Shravaka (Tib: nyan.thos.pa) literally means "hearer." These practitioners concentrate on renouncing the world and pacifying the emotions. Pratyekabuddha (Tib: rang.sangs.rgyas) literally means "solitary Buddha." They concentrate on individual liberation through examining the Twelve-fold Chain of Interdependent Origination and the basic Buddhist doctrines such as the Four Noble Truths, in order to achieve Arhathood.

Jewels, Three (Tib: dkon.mchog.gsum) These are the three objects of refuge: Buddha, Dharma, and Sangha.

Kalpa (Tib: bskal.pa) Like an eon, a kalpa is a very long but indefinite period of time. The general sense is that a kalpa is much longer than an eon, accounting for perhaps hundreds of millions of years.

Karma (Tib: las) *Action.* The law of karma is the doctrine of action and result. This holds that all experience down to minute details is the result of previous action, and all future conditions are determined by what is done in the present. Virtuous actions lead to better states of existence; nonvirtuous actions lead to suffering and unpleasant states.

Mahamudra (Tib: phyag.rgya.chen.po) *Great seal* or *great gesture.* This is the meditative tradition passed down especially by the Kagyu school from Vajradhara Buddha to Tilopa and down to the present lineage holders. It is a state in which all experiences are transformed into wisdom and skillful means. From the union of these arises the empty, luminous, and unimpeded experience of enlightenment.

Mahayana (Tib: theg.pa.chen.po) *Greater Vehicle.* This vehicle is founded on teachings presented by Shakyamuni on Vulture Peak in northern India to an assembly of Buddhas, Bodhisattvas, and Arhats. These teachings go beyond the individual liberation emphasized by the Hinayana schools and teach a greater vision based on the emptiness of all phenomena, great compassion for all sentient beings, and acknowledgement of the universal buddha-nature.

Mandala (Tib: dkyil.'khor) *Circle* or *sphere.* This is a symbolic representation of a meditation visualization, usually taking the form of a palace with one or more deities present. Mandalas are traditional offerings for one's guru and are often imagined to be limitless in size, number, and splendid qualities.

Mantra (Tib: sngags) Mantras are Sanskrit words or syllables expressing the essence of various energies. Mantra protects the concentration of mind and is always done in conjunction with visualization. which is performed according to the prescriptions of a sadhana explained by one's guru (see **Sadhana**).

Ngöndro (Tib: sngon.'gro) *Preliminary.* This is used to describe the four extraordinary practices traditionally done at the beginning of a student's Dharma life. They consist of 111,111 each of refuge and prostrations, Dorje Sempa mantras, mandala offerings, and prayers to one's guru or lama; their purpose is to purify the body, speech, and mind of the individual in order to realize the Mahamudra stage.

Nidanas (Tib: rten.'brel.bcu.gnyis) Refers to the twelve links of interdependent origination. In the Mahayana tradition especially, meditating on this teaching that all actions and events are interconnected is considered to be an antidote to ignorance.

Nirvana (Tib: mya.ngan.las.'das.ba) *Beyond suffering.* This term, in the context of the Buddha's teachings, refers to a state of being which is quite different from ordinary bliss. Nirvana is not a temporary cessation of daily problems, but rather a state which is beyond even the causes of those problems.

Pratekyabuddha See **Hinayana**

Preta (Tib: yi.dags) *Hungry ghost.* The term *preta* is ordinarily used to refer only to beings who abide in the preta realm (one of the six realms of cyclic existence), however, this term can also refer to a being in any realm who is obsessed with objects of desire such as food and drink.

Roots, Three (Tib: rtsa.gsum) The Three Roots in which the Vajrayana practitioner takes refuge (in addition to the Three Jewels) are the blessing root (the guru), the accomplishment root (the yidam), and the activity root (the dharma protectors).

Sadhana (Tib: sgrub.thabs) *Means of Accomplishment.* Any Vajrayana ritual that sets out the visualizations and recitations for a particular meditation practice.

Samadhi (Tib: ting.nge.'dzin) This describes a one-pointed involvement in meditation where the object of meditation and the practitioner are experienced as inseparable and indistinguishable. While there are many kinds of samadhi, it is important to note that the term does not imply anything about the practitioner's realization or accomplishment.

Samsara (Tib: 'khor.ba) Samsara is the cycle of rebirth, the wheel of existence, which arises out of ignorance and is marked by suffering.

Sangha (Tib: dge.'dun) In the broadest sense, the term refers to the whole community of practitioners from monks, nuns, and lay people to the assembly of enlightened bodhisattvas. The Sangha is one of the three objects of refuge. (See **Jewels, Three**)

Shamatha (Tib: zhi.gnas) *Calm abiding.* This term denotes both a method of meditation to achieve tranquility and the meditative state that is its result.

Shravaka See **Hinayana**

Shunyata (Tib: stong.pa.nyid) This is the doctrine that all concepts and phenomena are empty of any reality and that self and other are egoless. Shunyata is like space, unborn and unceasing.

Sutra (Tib: mdo) This refers to texts in the Buddhist canon attributed to Shakyamuni Buddha. They are usually dialogues between the Buddha and one or more of his disciples, elaborating a particular topic.

Tantra (Tib: rgyud) This word has many meanings, but essentially, it refers to those systems of meditation described in the root texts of Vajrayana. Tantra means continuity. This refers to the continuity maintained throughout one's practice, from the basic ground or foundation, along the path, and through to complete fruition of the practice.

Vajrayana (Tib: rdo.rje.theg.pa) *Diamond* or *Indestructible Vehicle.* This vehicle is based on the teachings of Shakyamuni manifesting in the form of Vajradhara, the Dharmakaya Buddha. They consist mostly of oral and secret teachings passed from teacher to disciple. There are two classes of these oral teachings, one for gifted students capable of instantaneous enlightenment and a second delineating a graded path of instructions in which the student passes from one stage to the next, coming gradually to enlightenment. Because the Vajrayana presents the practitioner with the actual fruition of wakefulness and suchness, it is called the quick path. It is said that one practicing the Vajrayana can achieve Buddhahood in a single lifetime.

Vipasyana (Tib: lhag.mthong) *Seeing beyond; superior or excellent seeing; insight.* This is a meditative technique which identifies and analyzes the patterns of the mind and the world it projects, achieving a state of clear-seeing which expands into perfect knowledge.

Yana (Tib: theg.pa) *Path, vehicle, way.*

BIBLIOGRAPHY

Guenther, Herbert V., trans. *Jewel Ornament of Liberation* by sGam.po.pa. Boulder, Shambala, 1971.

McLeod, Kenneth, trans. *The Chariot for Travelling the Path to Freedom*. San Francisco, Kagyu Dharma, 1985.

McLeod, Kenneth, trans. *Writings of Kalu Rinpoche*. Vancouver, Kagyu Kunkhyab Chuling, 1976.

The Crystal Mirror. New York, Kagyu Thubten Choling, 1982.

DEDICATION

Whereby sentient beings who are tormented by the three kinds of suffering recognize the condition of limitless samsaric suffering and the state of Buddhahood—the nature of the Five Wisdoms and the Four Bodies—in the continuum, they apply a small amount of practice in their mind streams through deep faith and compassion, the two kinds of precious Bodhicitta, and the profound generation and completion stages. May they, having sown each seed of liberation, come to obtain the level of Buddhahood step by step.

With only this intention and also through this presentation of whatever is remembered of the essential instructions which are taught from the sutras and tantras, may all beings who will touch, remember, hear or see this work be liberated from the ocean of samsaric suffering.

Thus I, Kalu Rinpoche, the yogi of the royal domain, who have acquired faith in the tradition of Dharma that is not bound in sectarianism, have spoken. May there be favorable and auspicious prospect!

Mahakala
Painting by Cynthia Moku